DEMON DRAWINGS

RC Miller

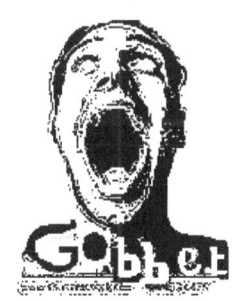

First published in 2014 by

goββετ press
in association with gobbet magazine

First edition
ISBN: 978-1499774177

Printed in the USA.

Some of these images first appeared in New Dead Families, and Mutantres.

CONTENTS

Demon Drawings

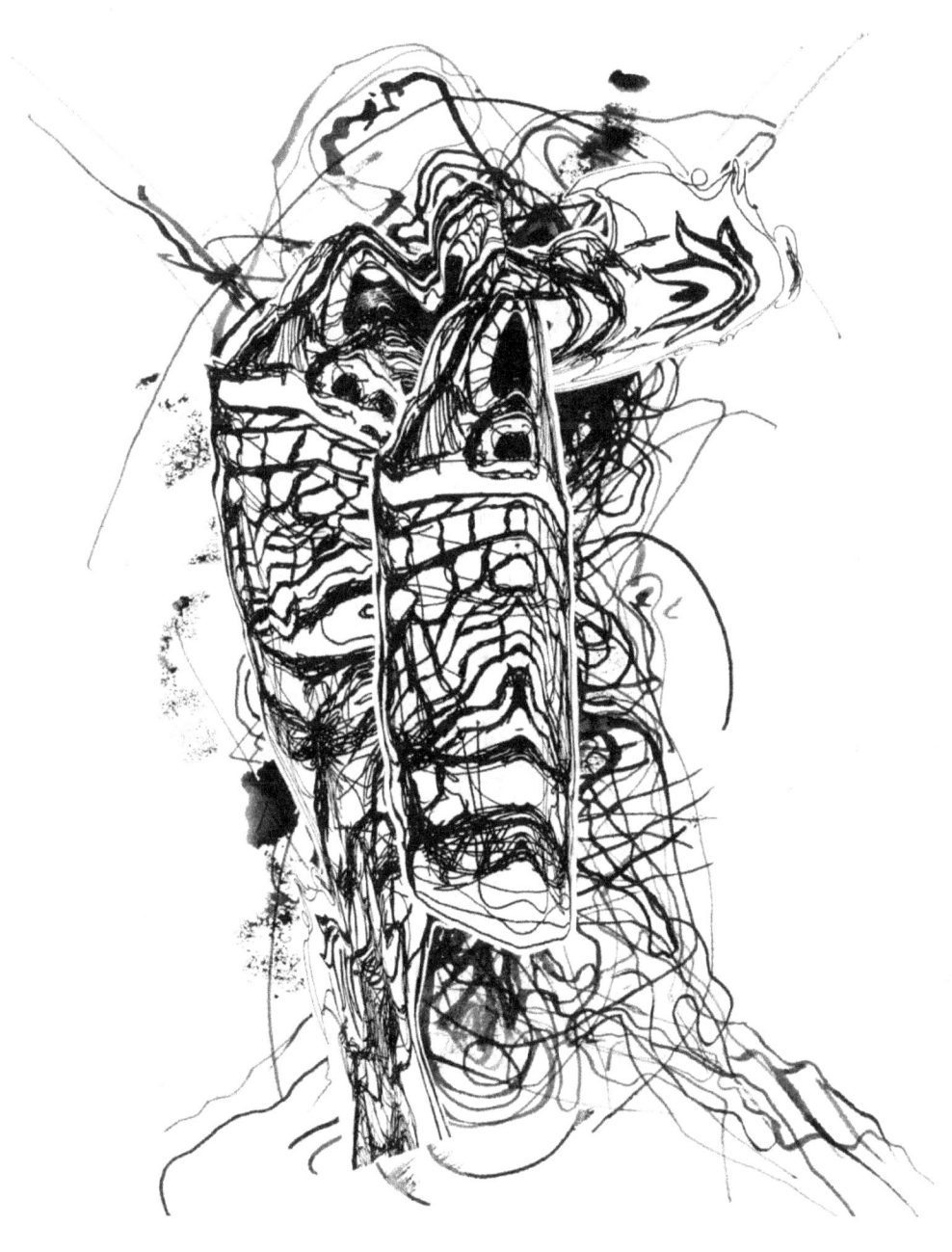

ACAPELLA

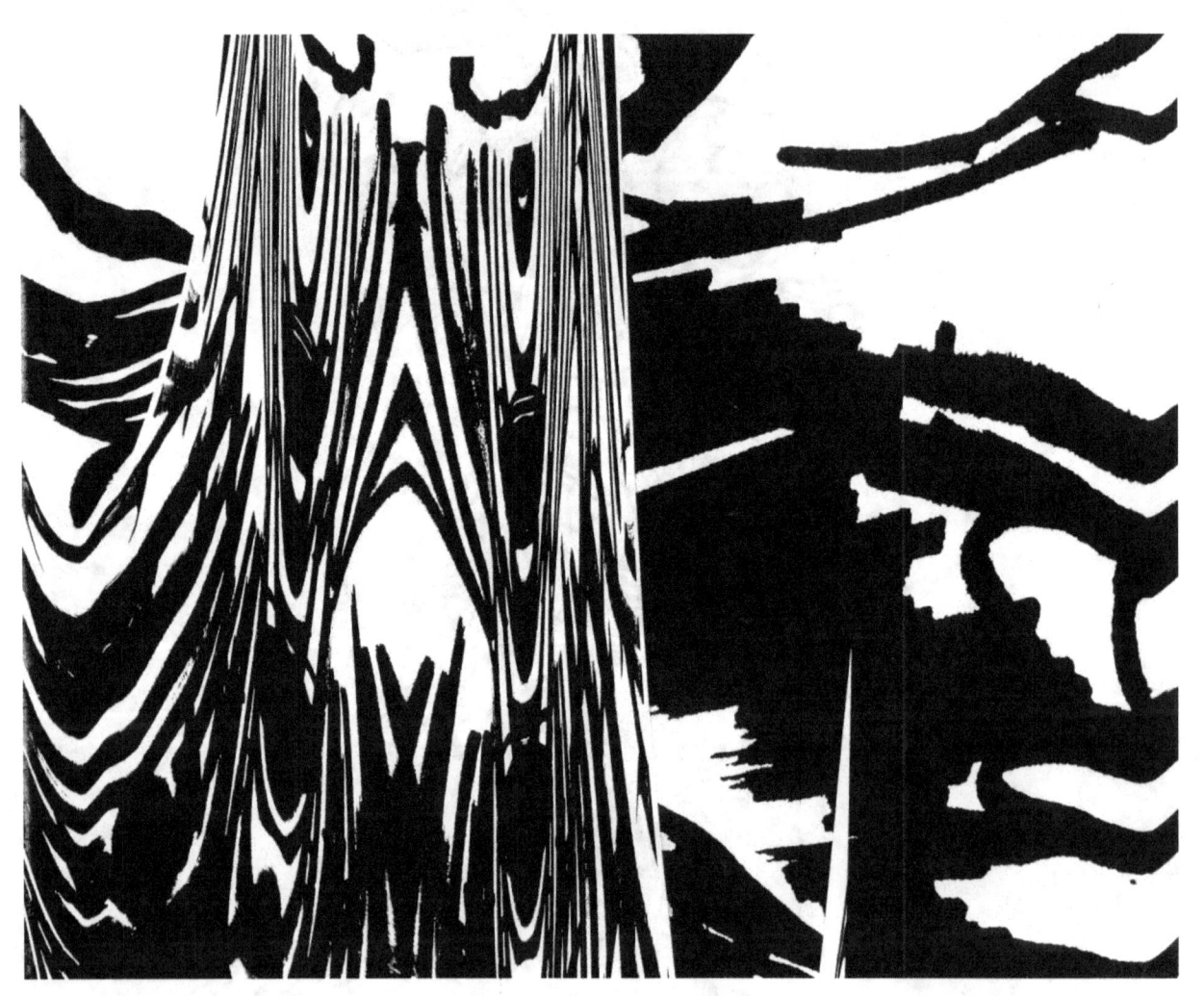

ALTARPIECE

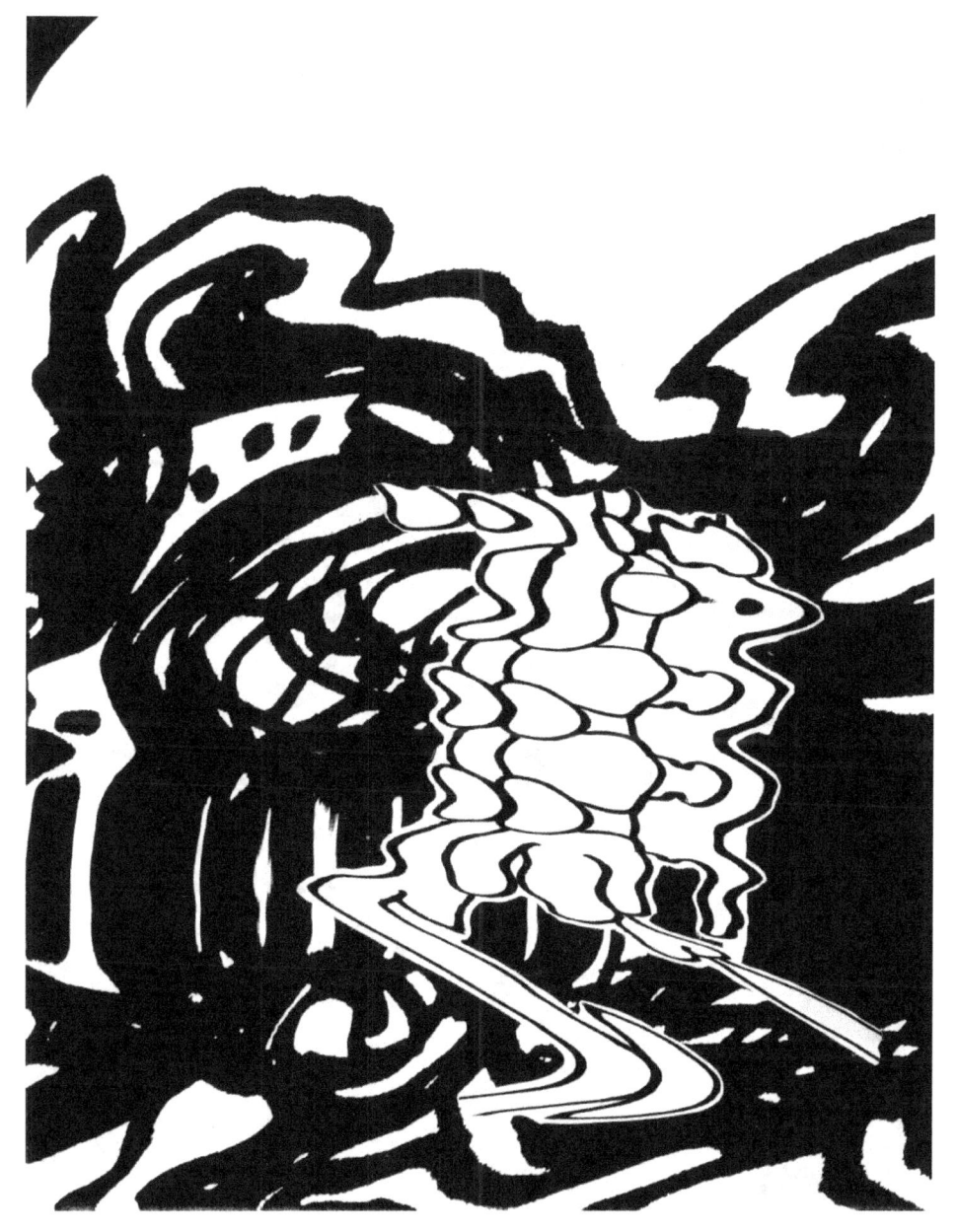

ASTRONAUT

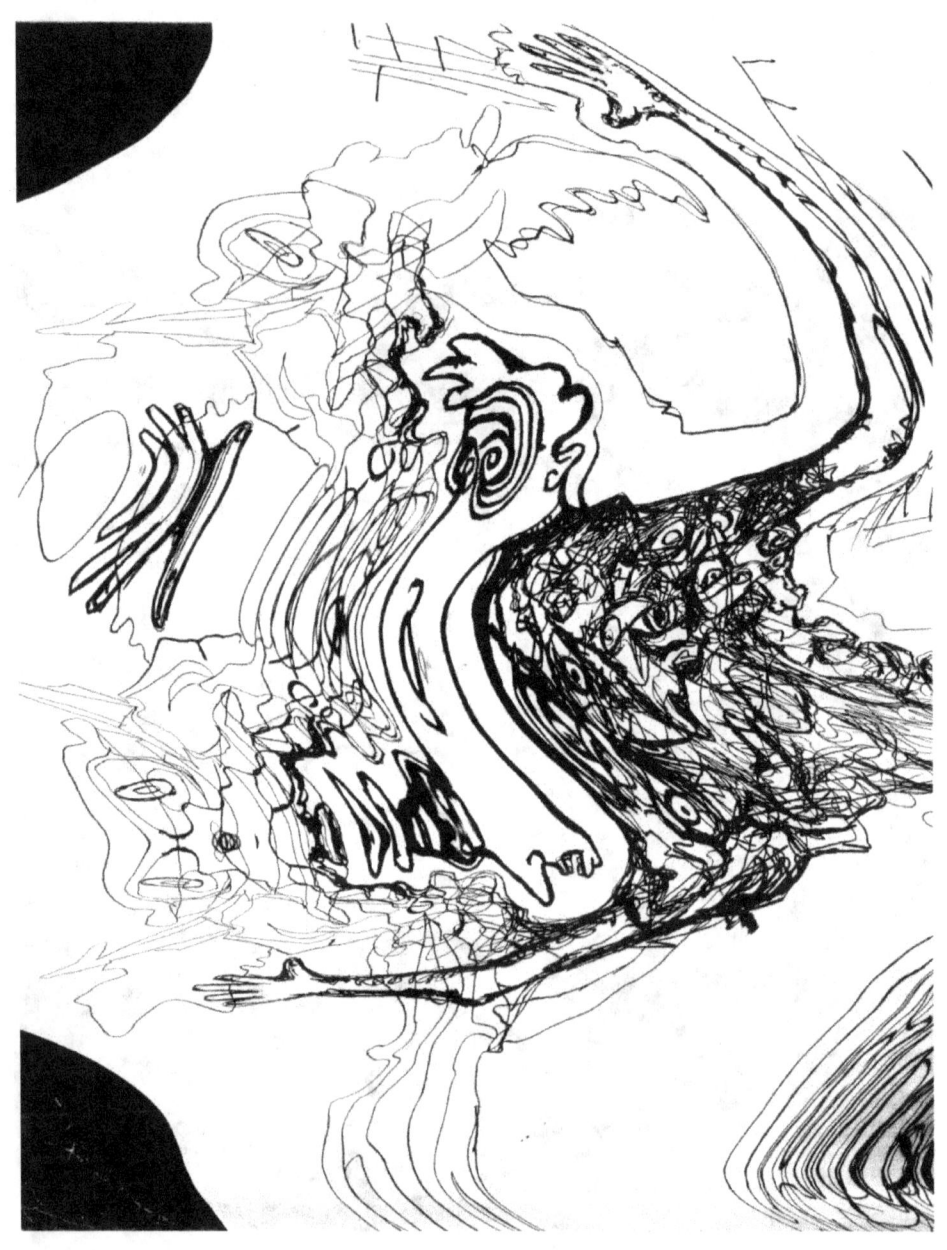

BARN DAYS

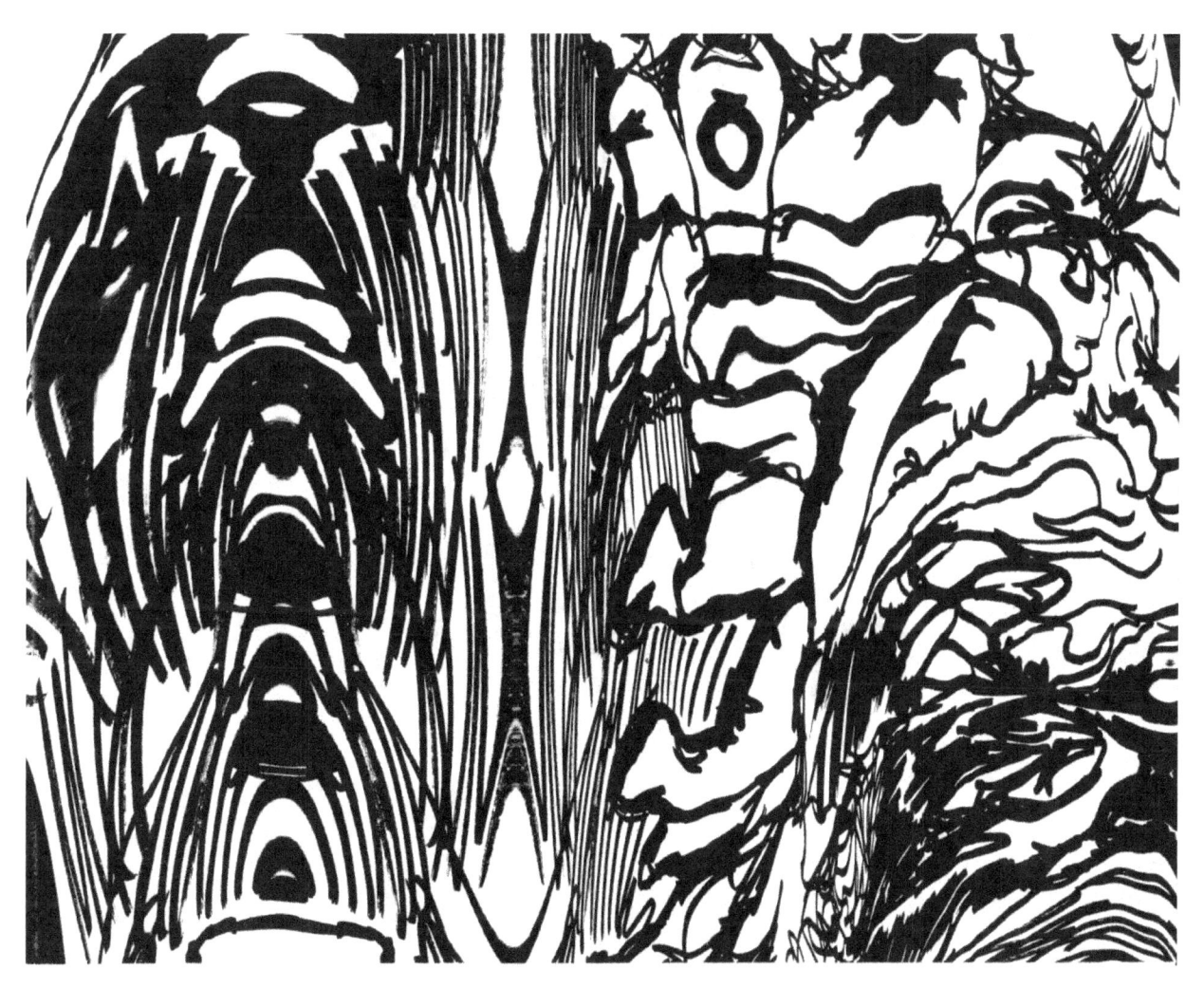

BEACON

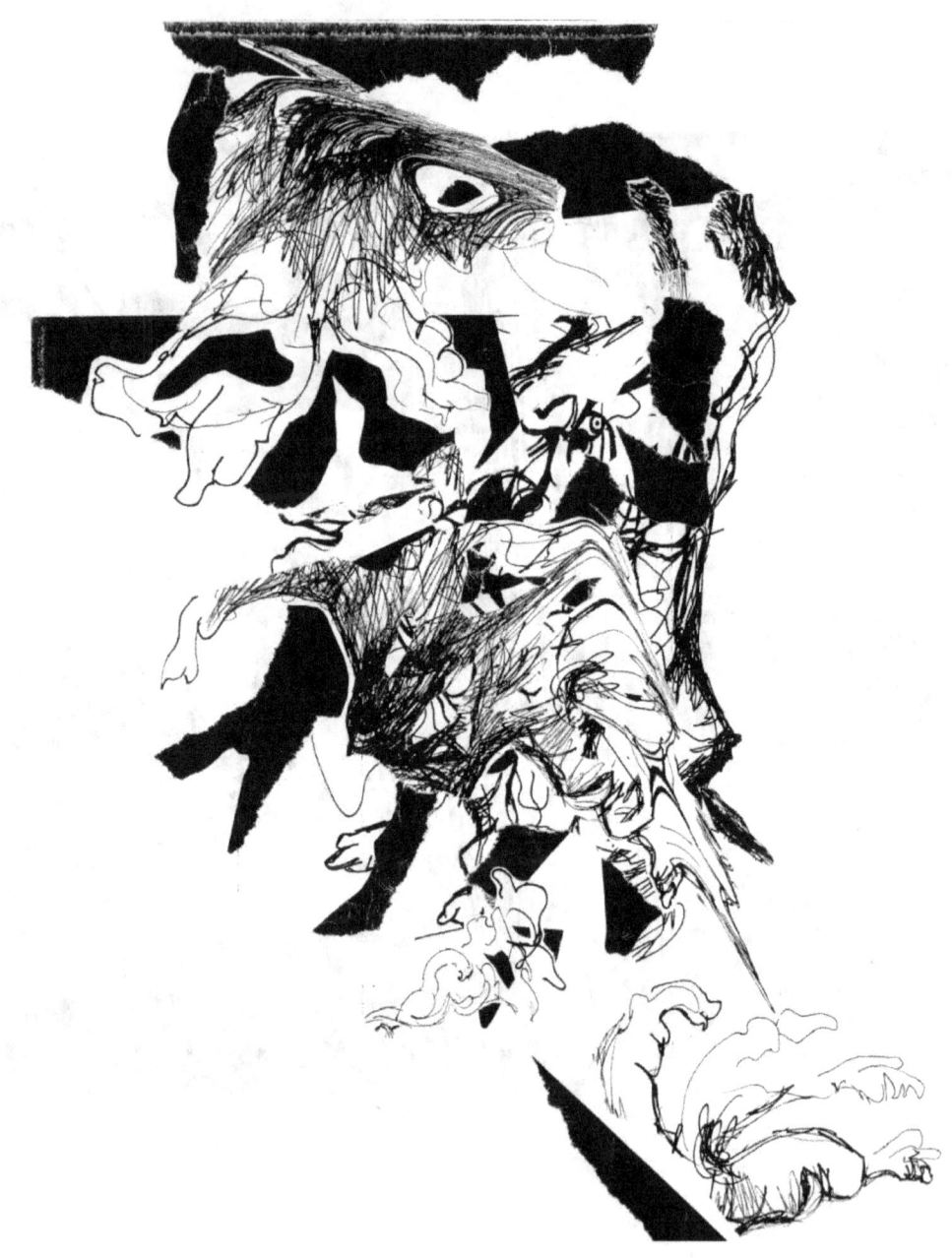

BEARER

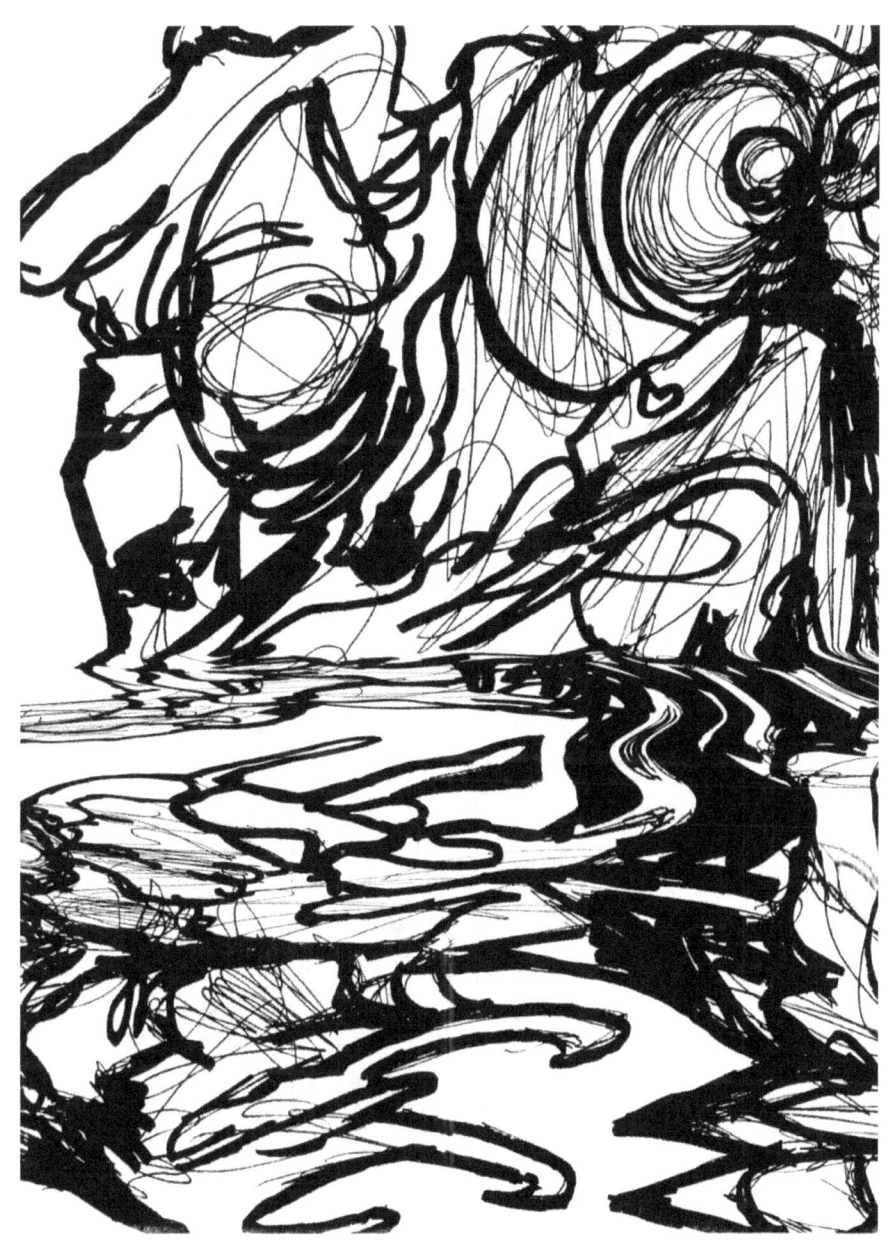

BICUSPID

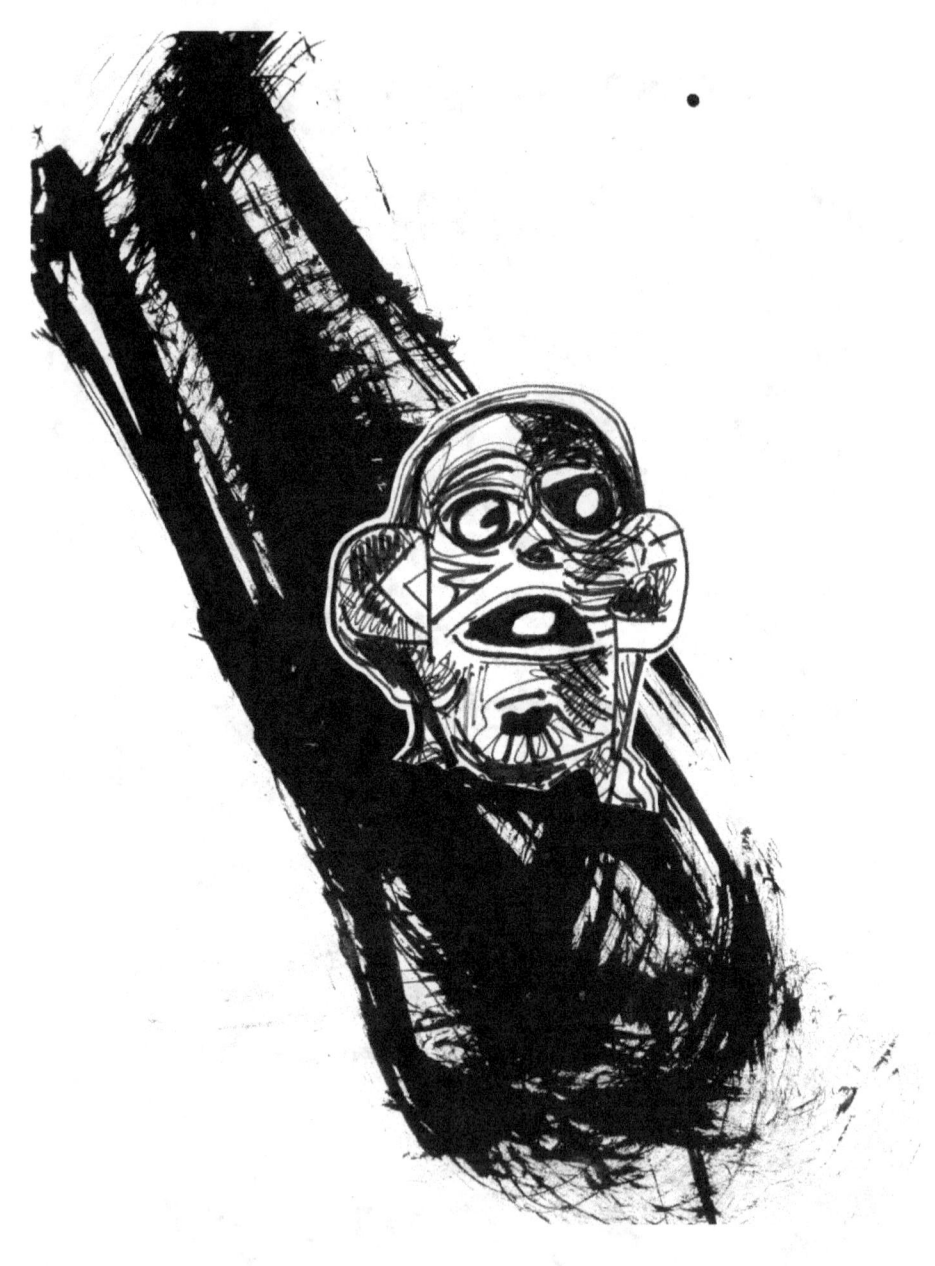

BLACK DICK

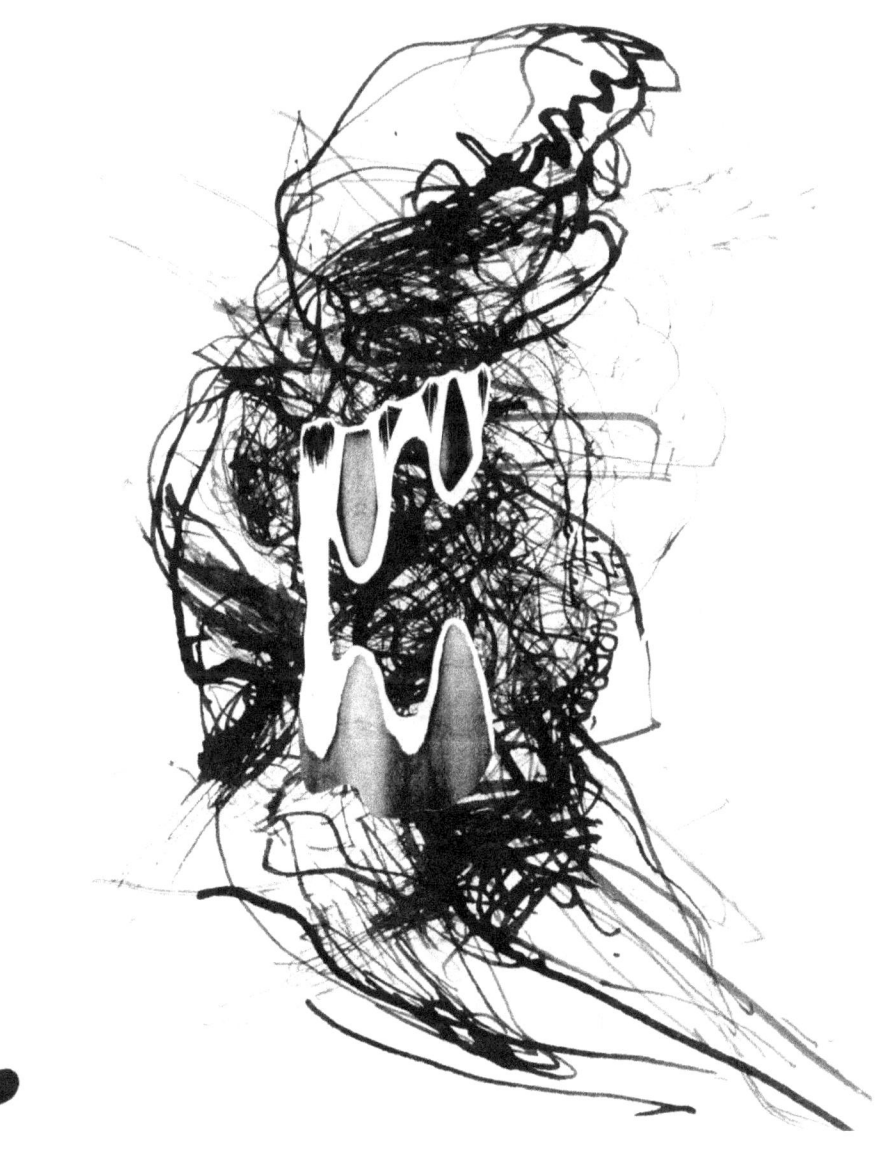

CATHOLICIZED

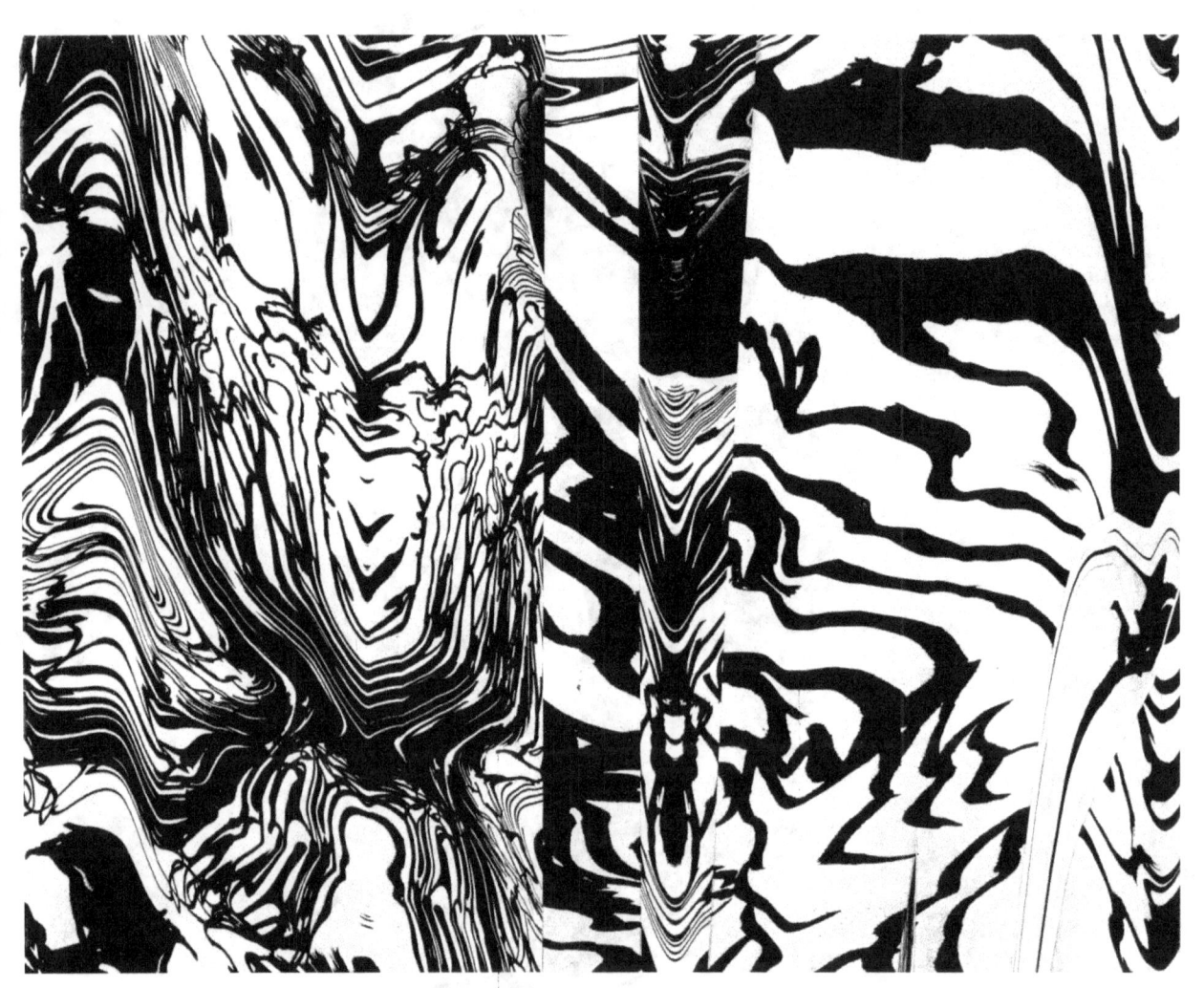

CLAMMY LAND

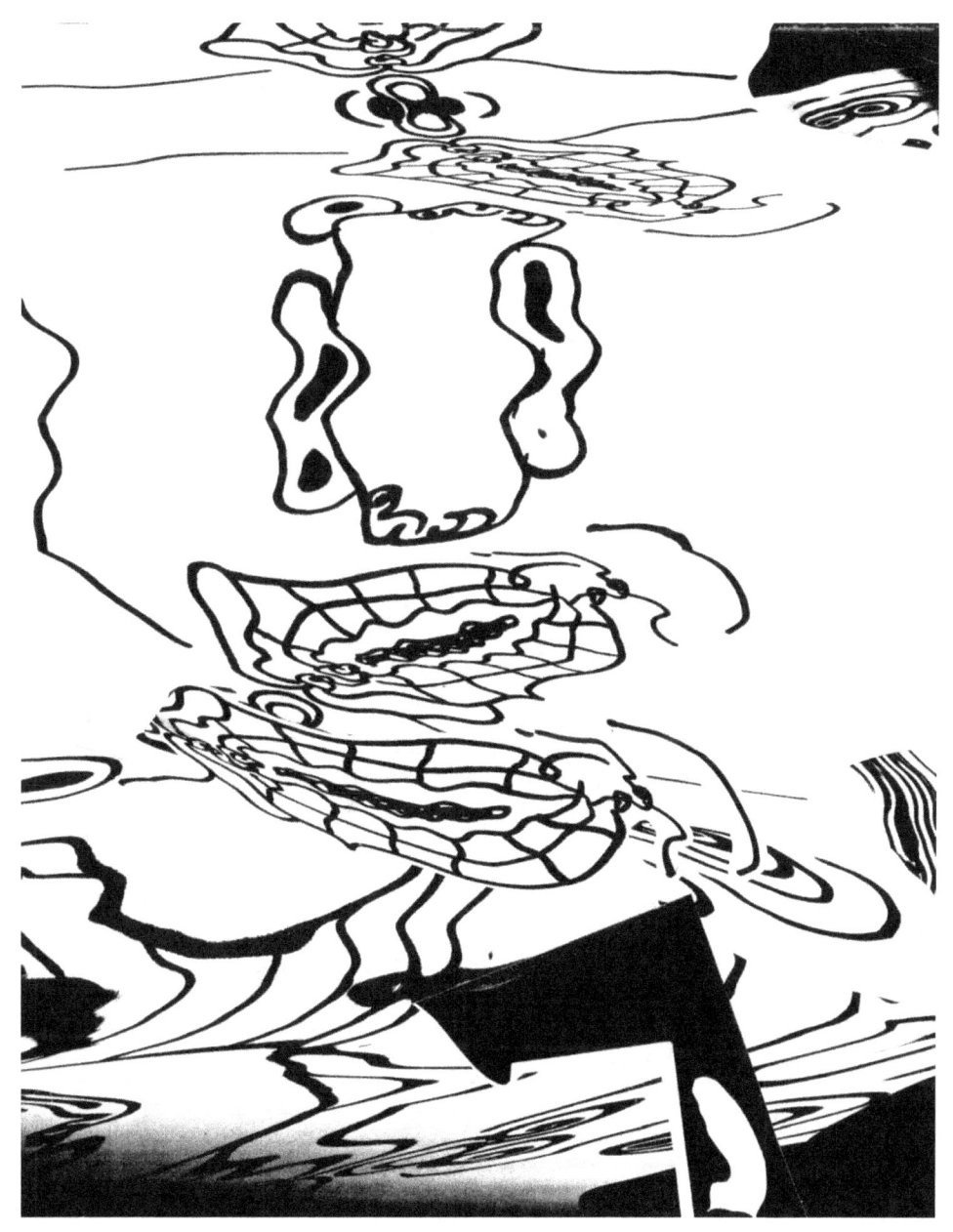

DAIRY DEMON

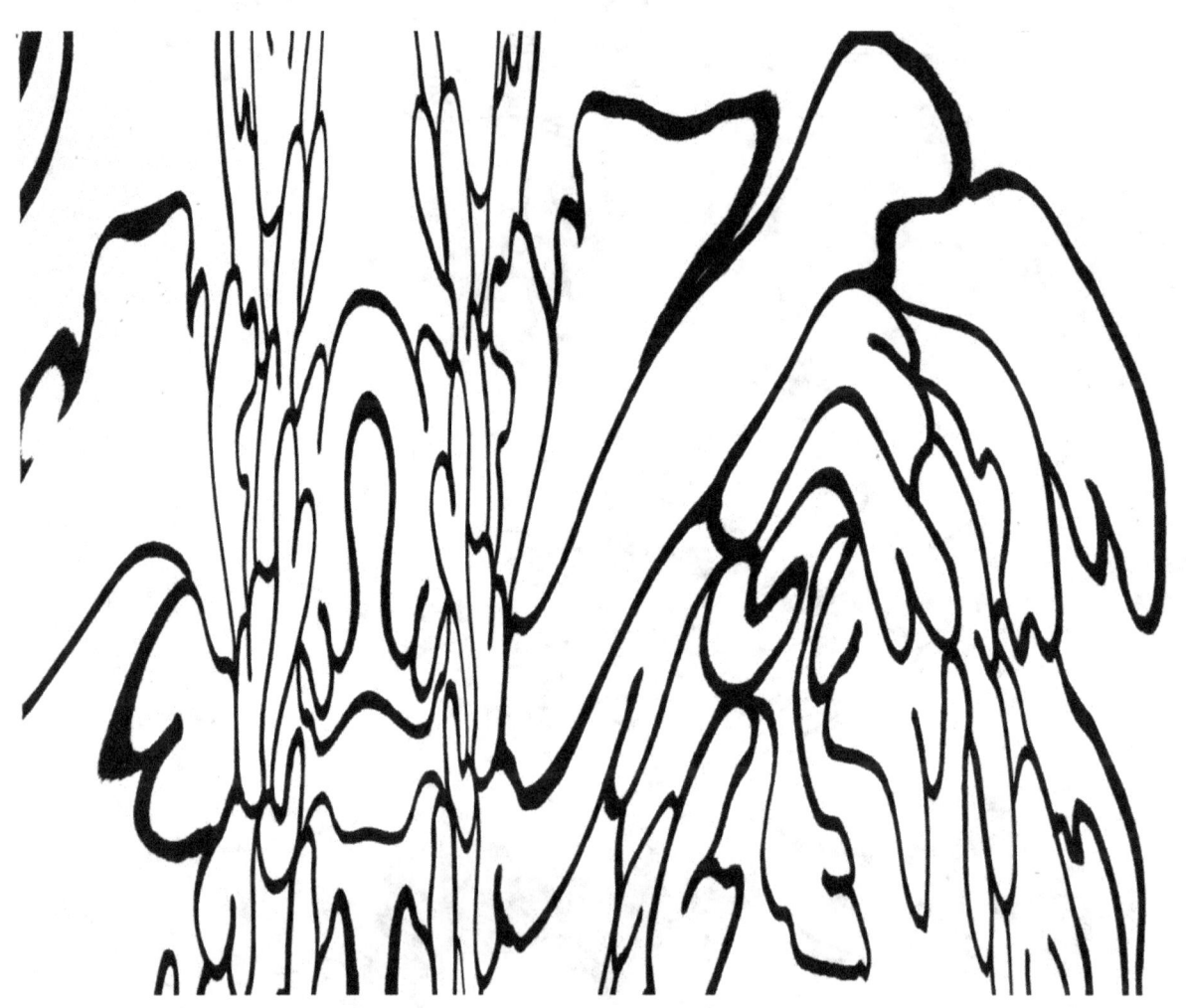

DAMMIT DEMON

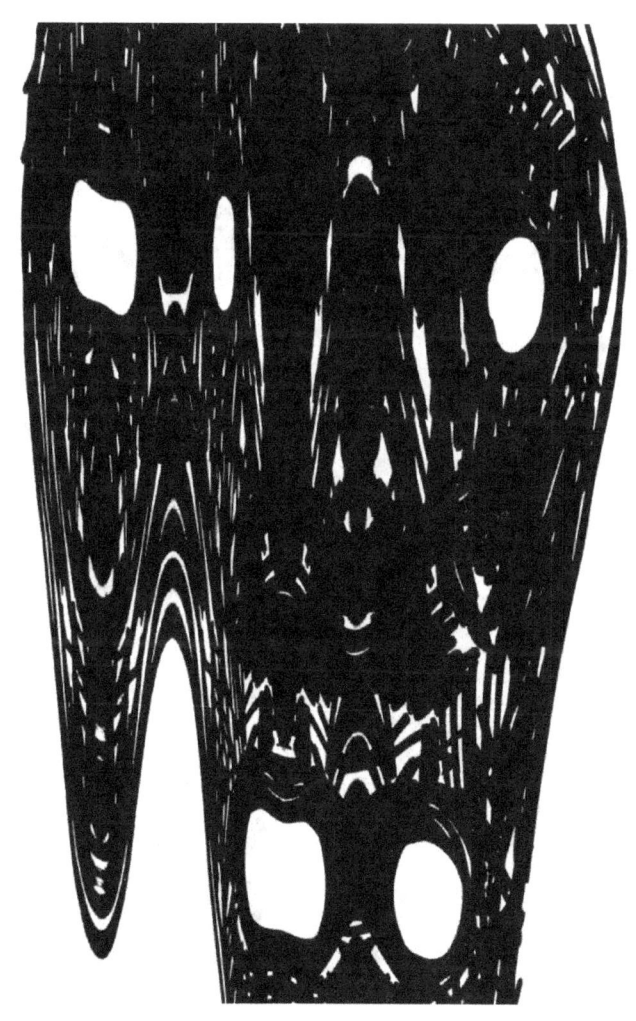

DATA DEMON

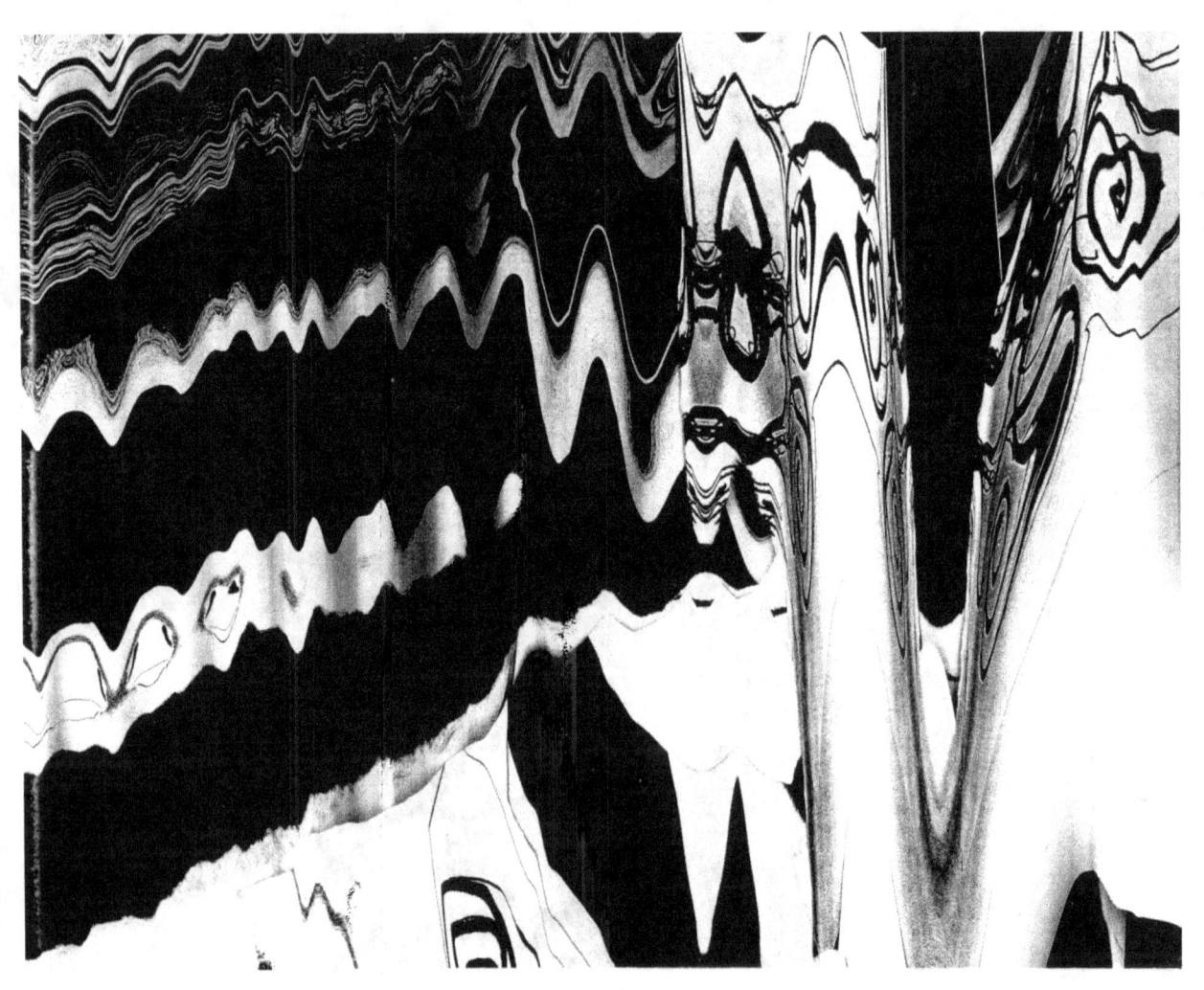

DATELESS DEMON

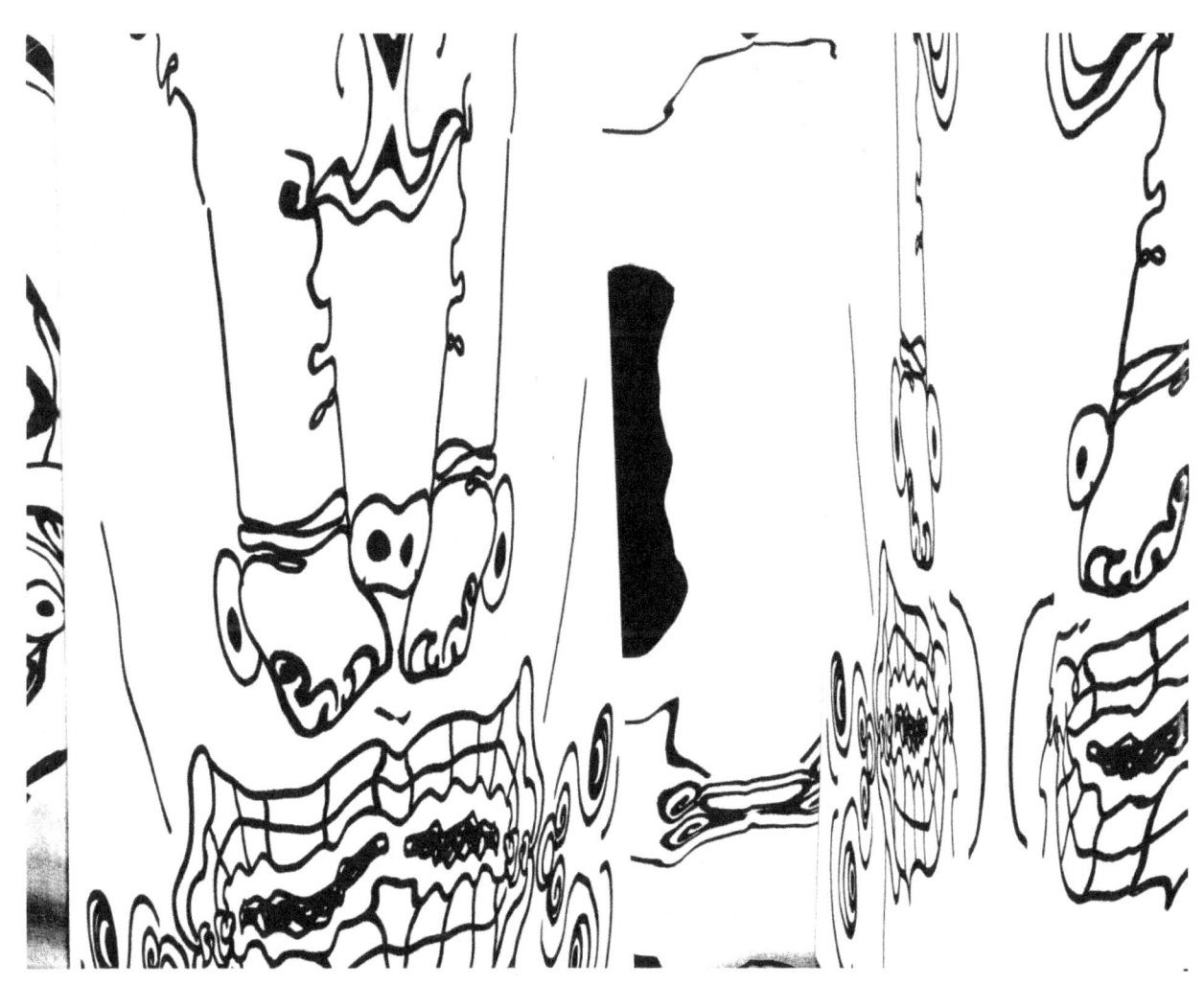

DENTAL FLOSS DEMON

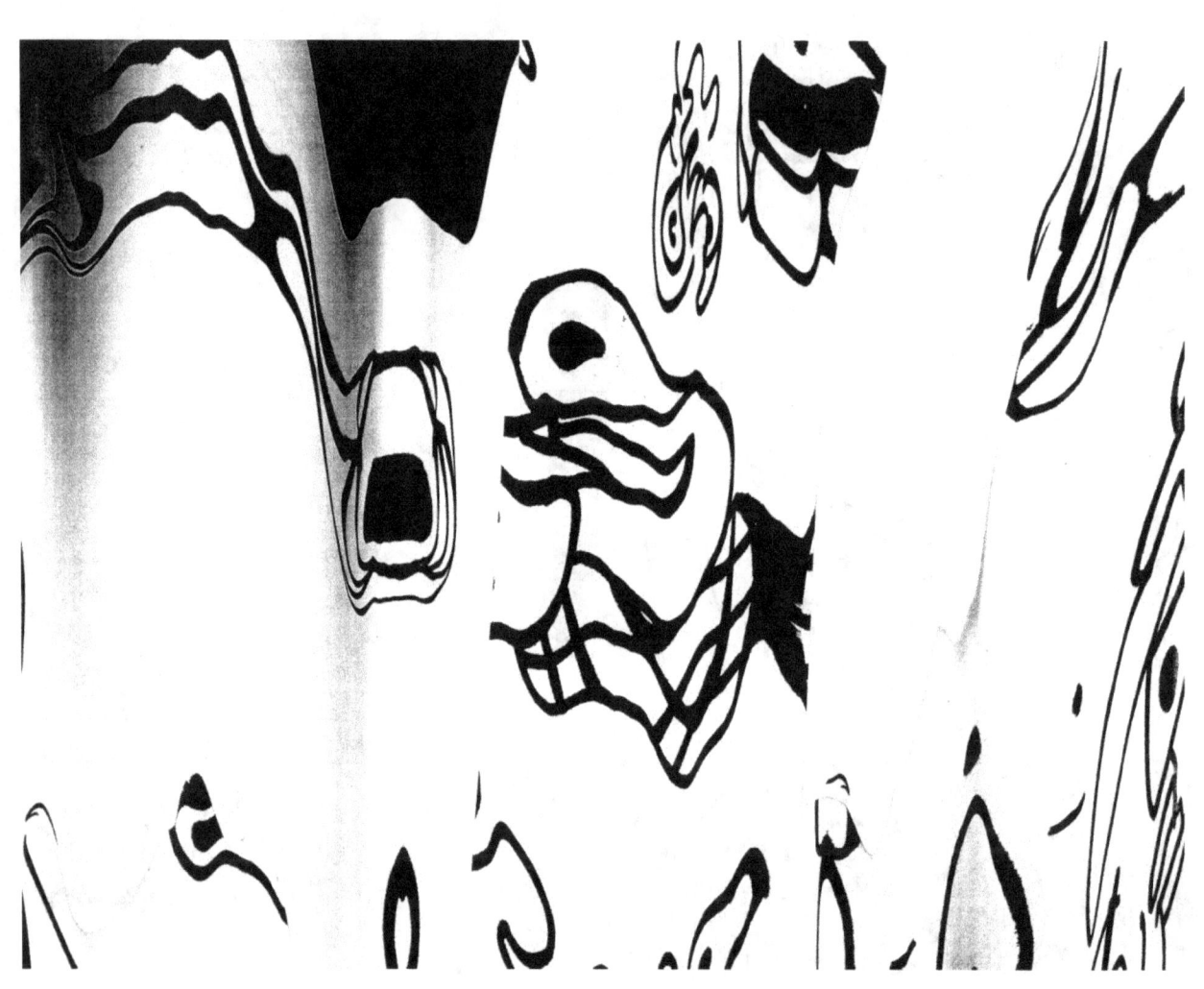

DEPENDABLE DEMON

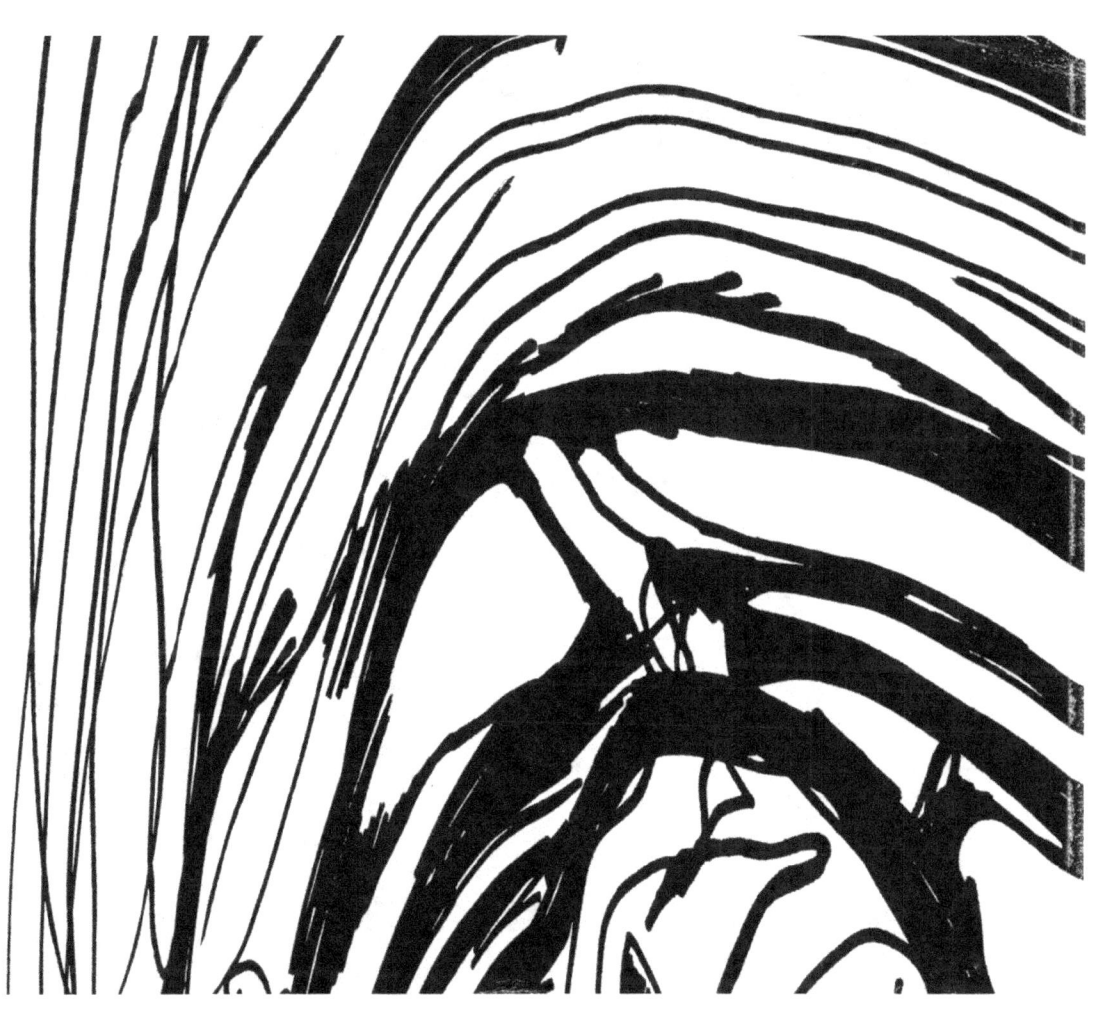

DESCRAMBLER DEMON

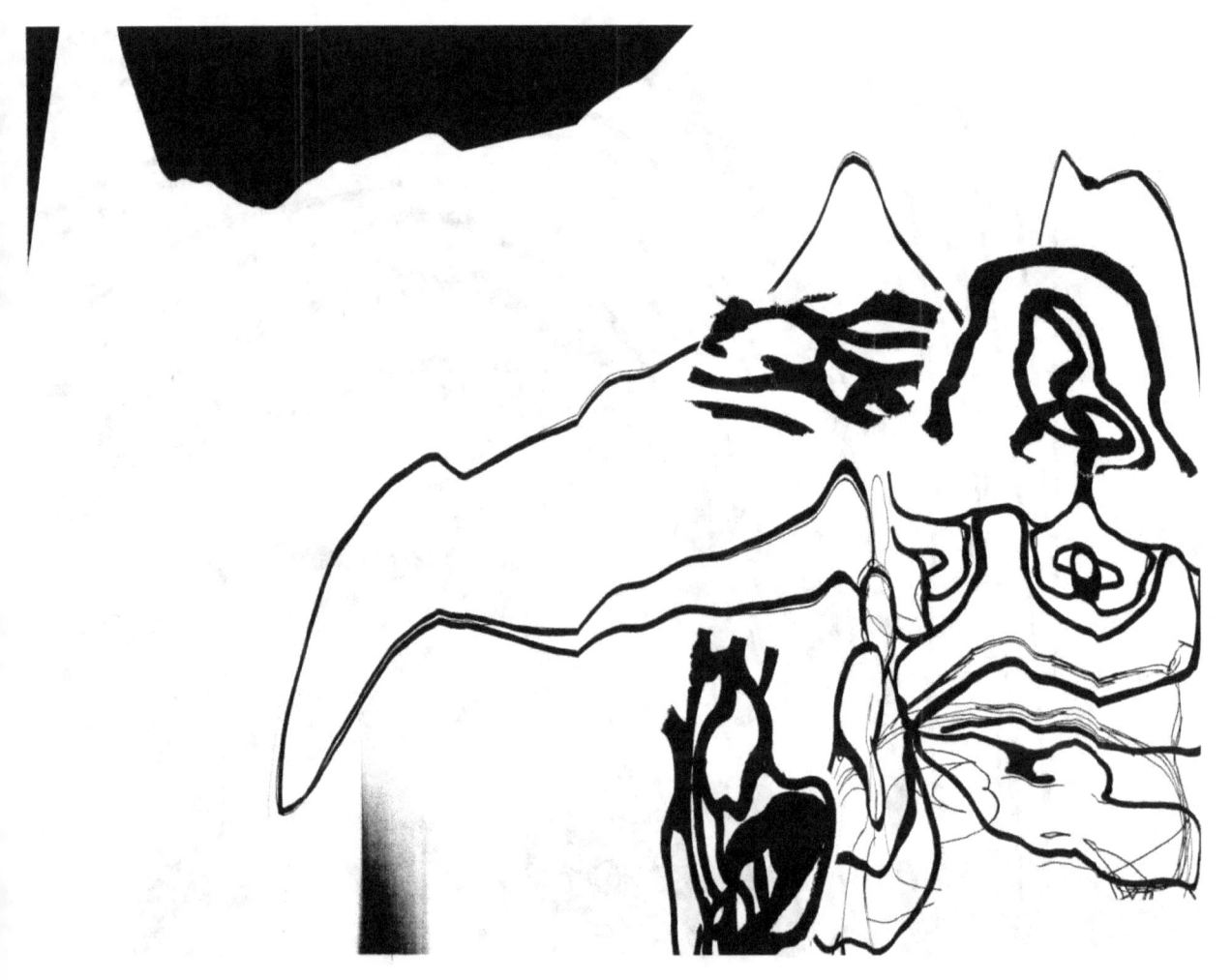

DETACHABLE DEMON

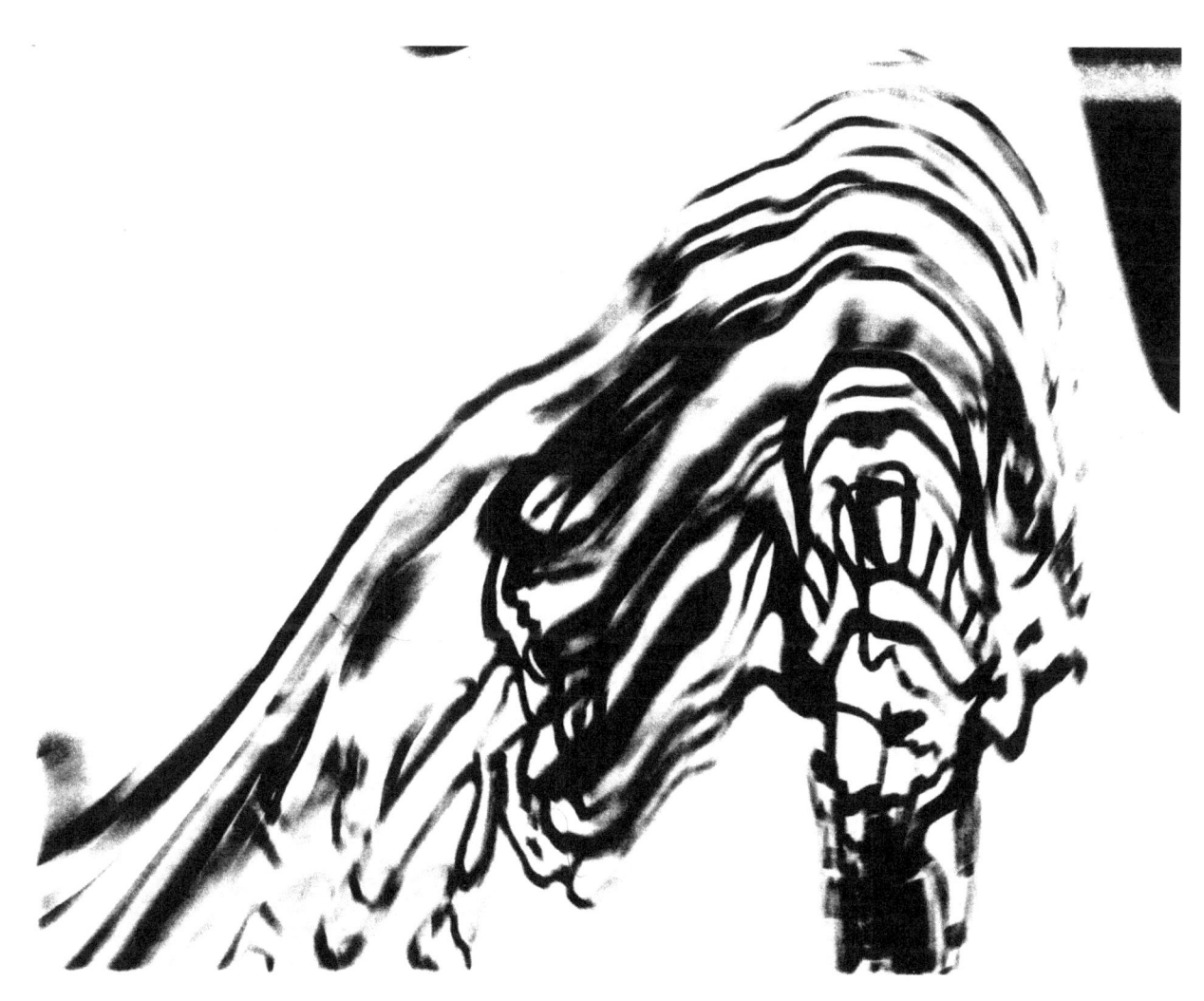

DETERMINISM DEMON

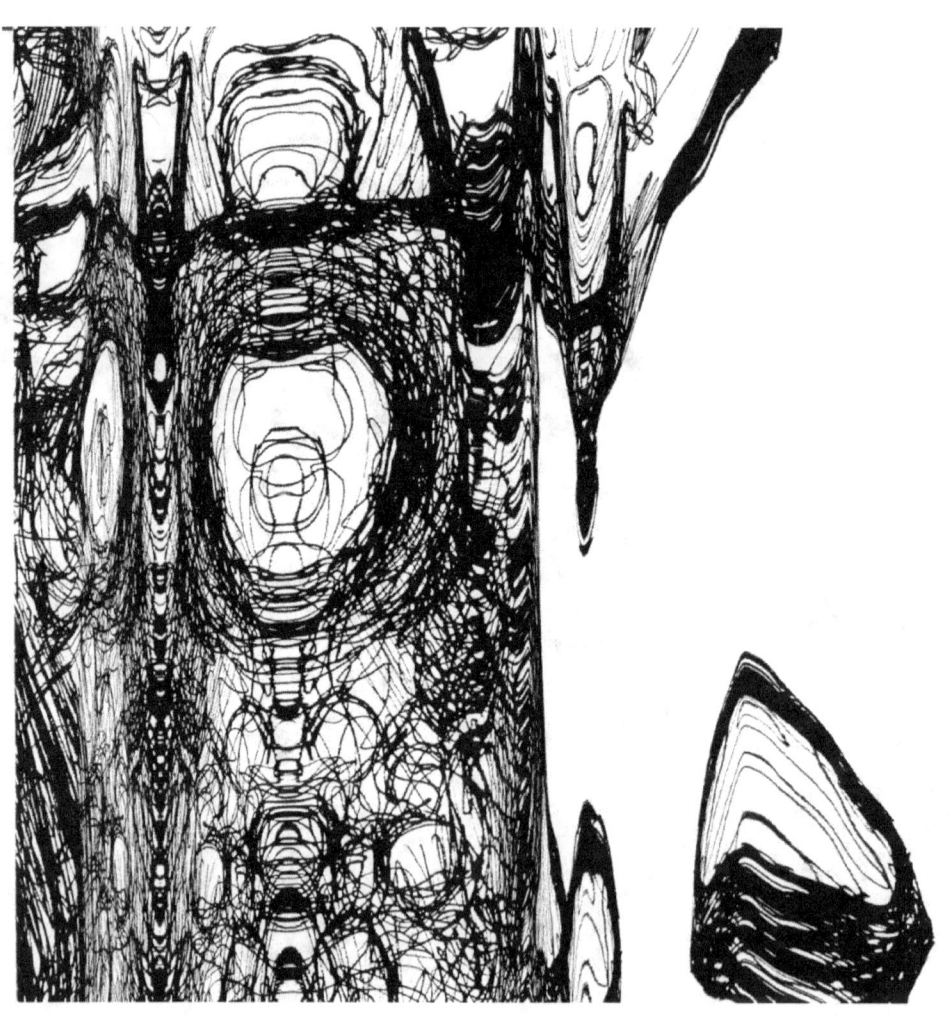

DETHRONED DEMON

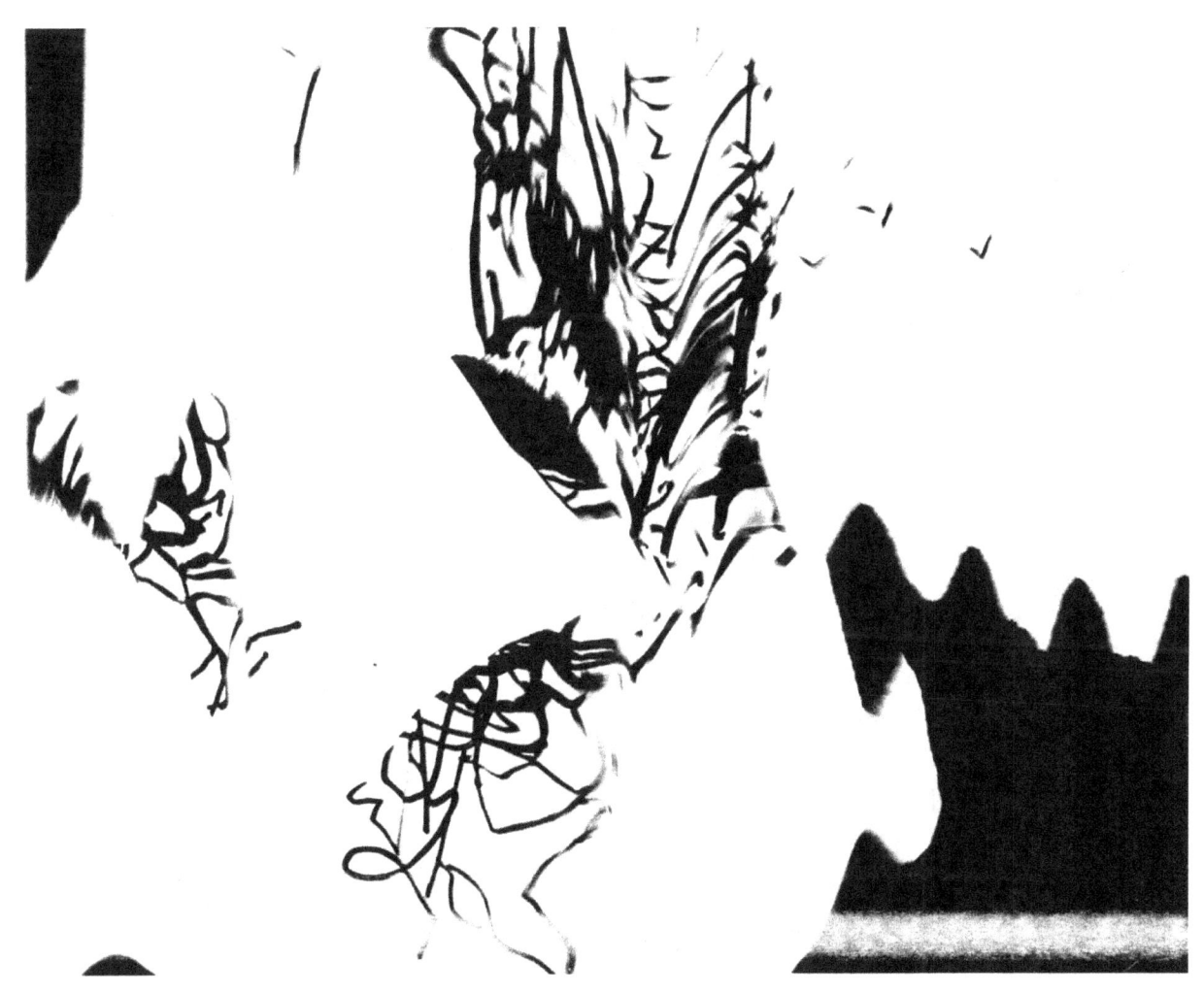

DETOXED DEMON

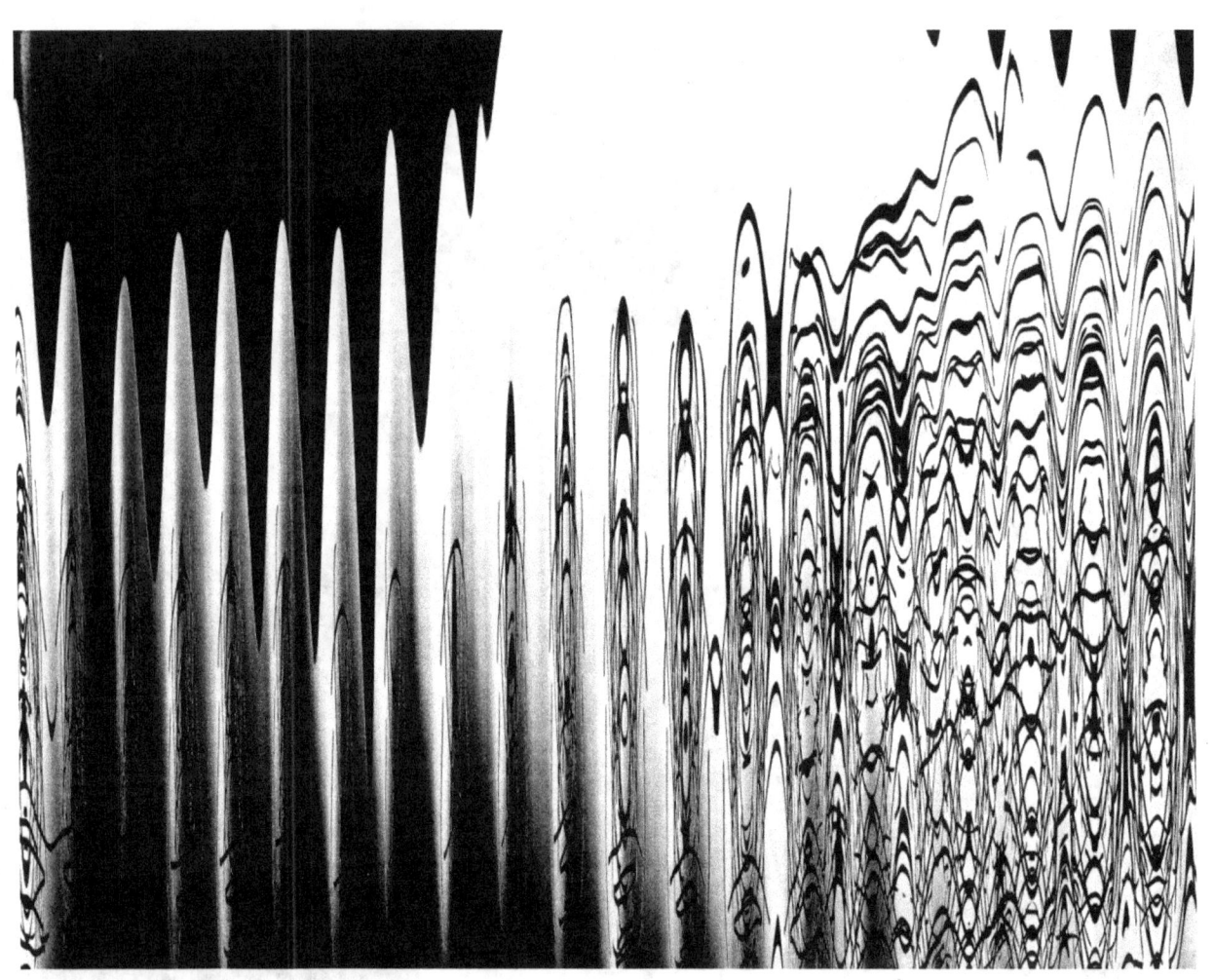

DETRITUS DEMON

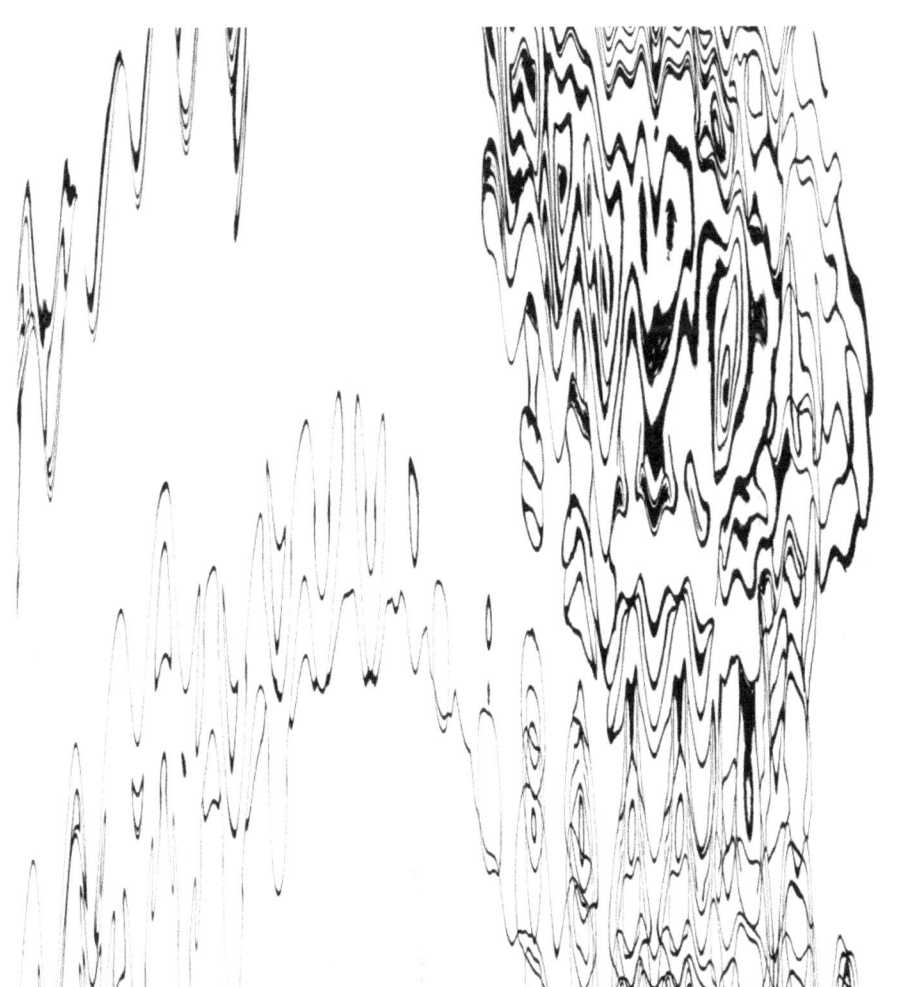

DEVOTED DEMON

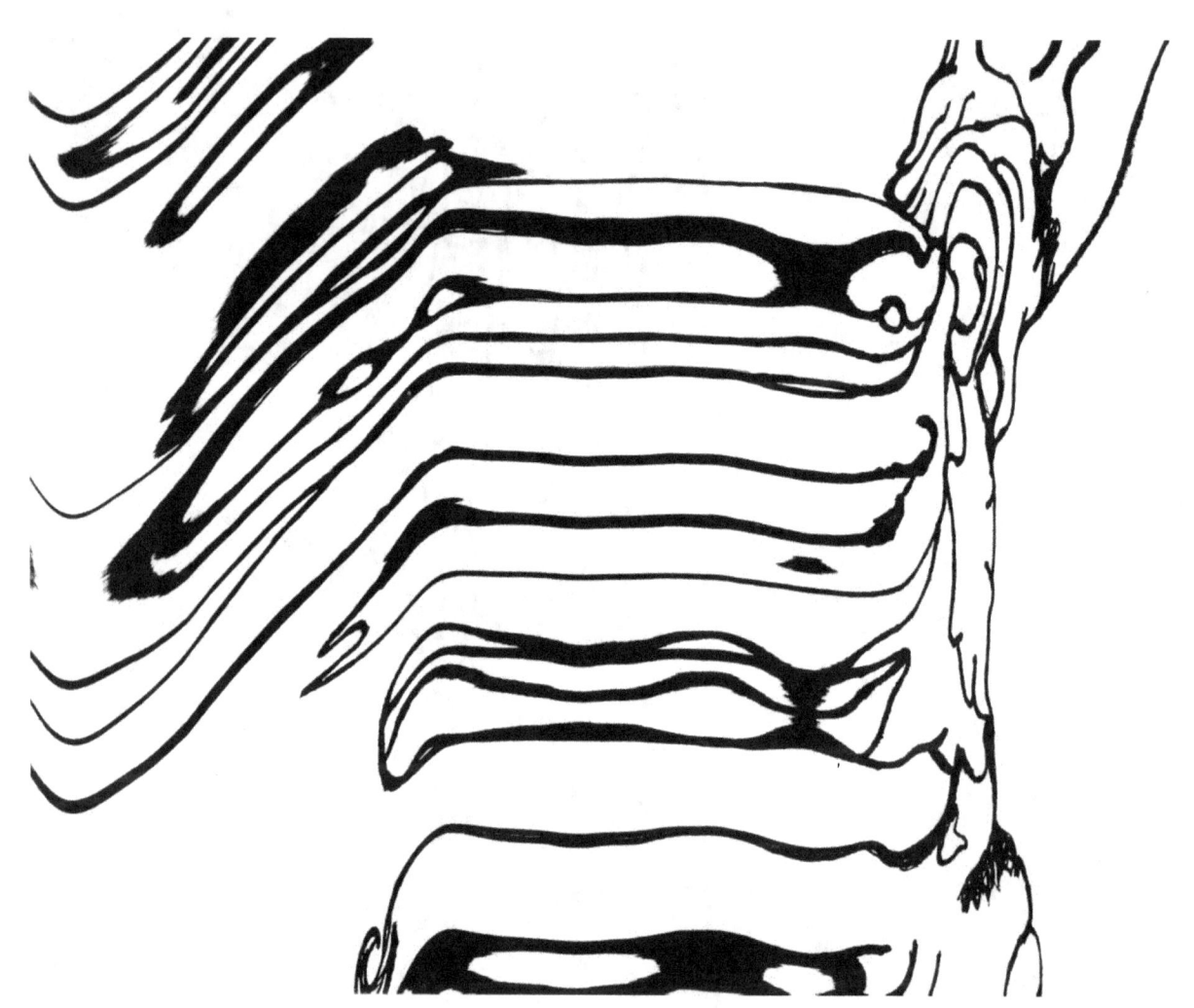

DIAPHRAGM DEMON

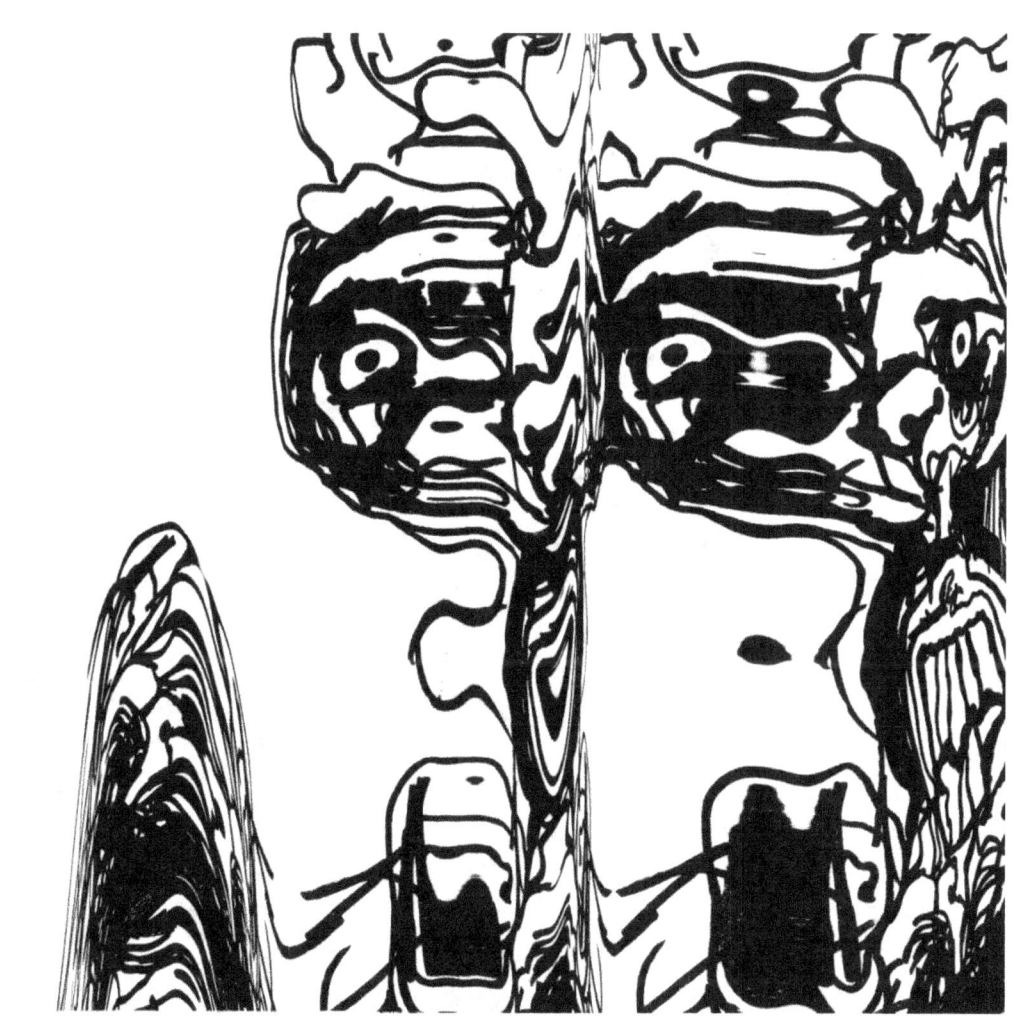

DIBS DEMON

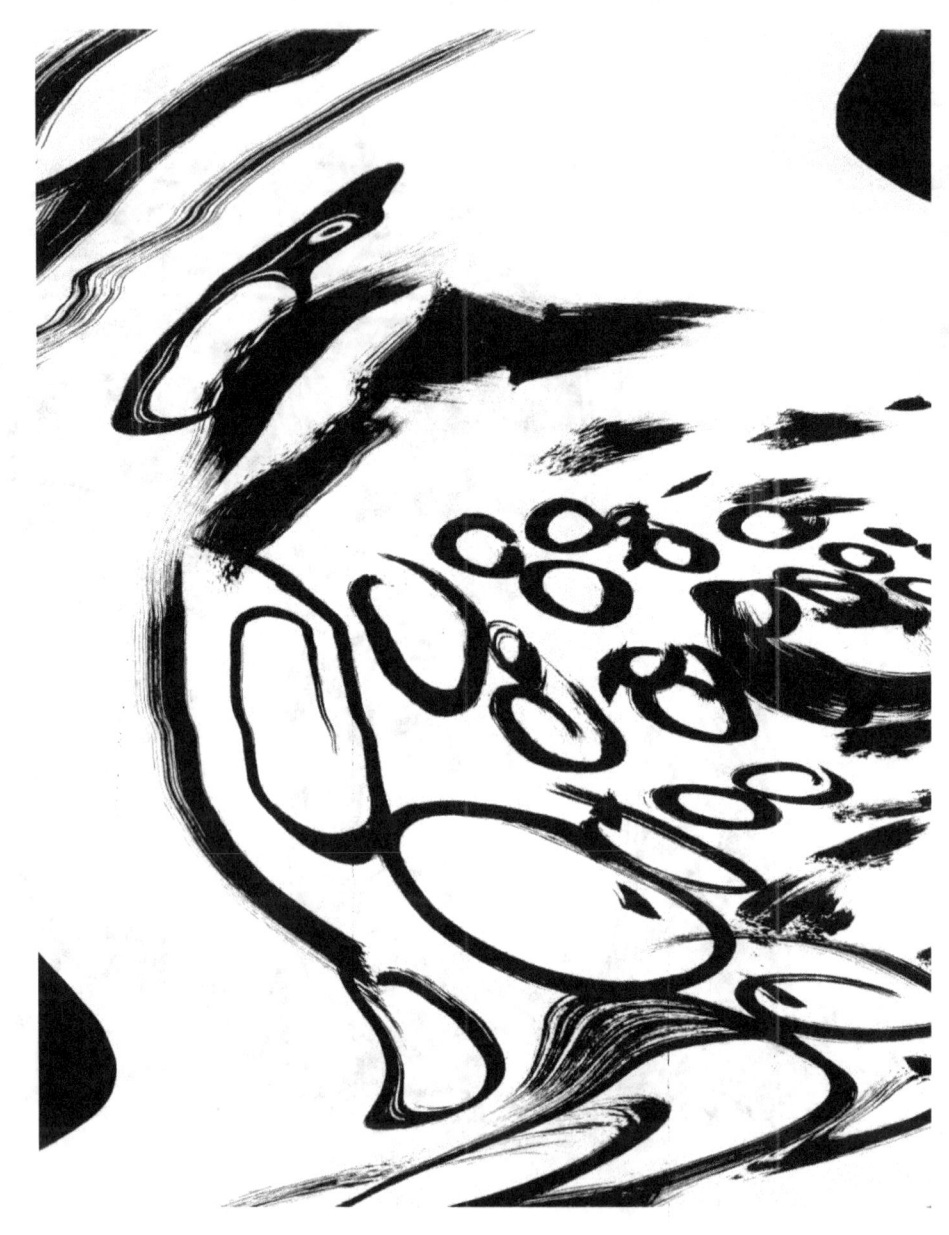

DIGESTED DEMON

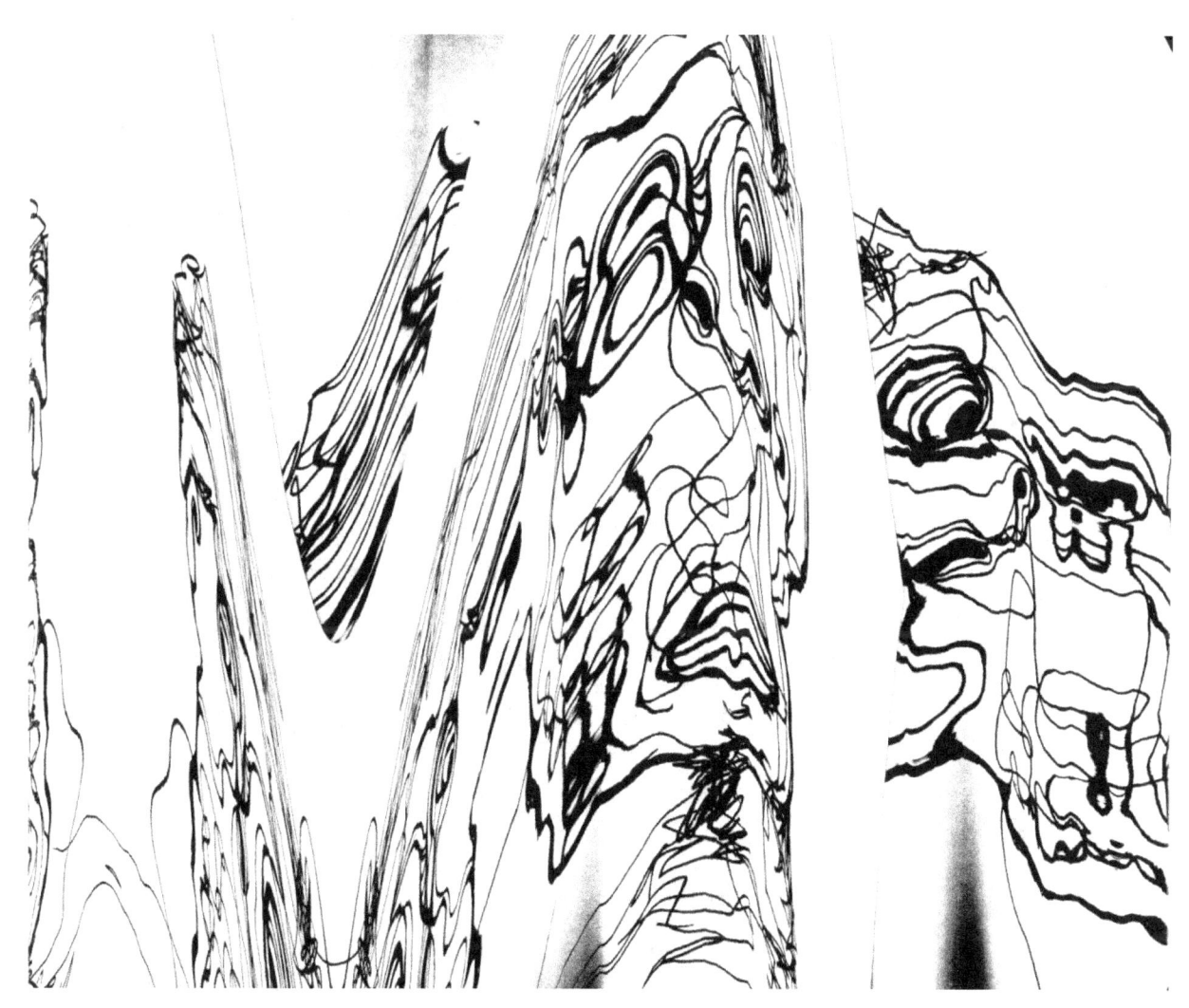

DILAPIDATED DEMON

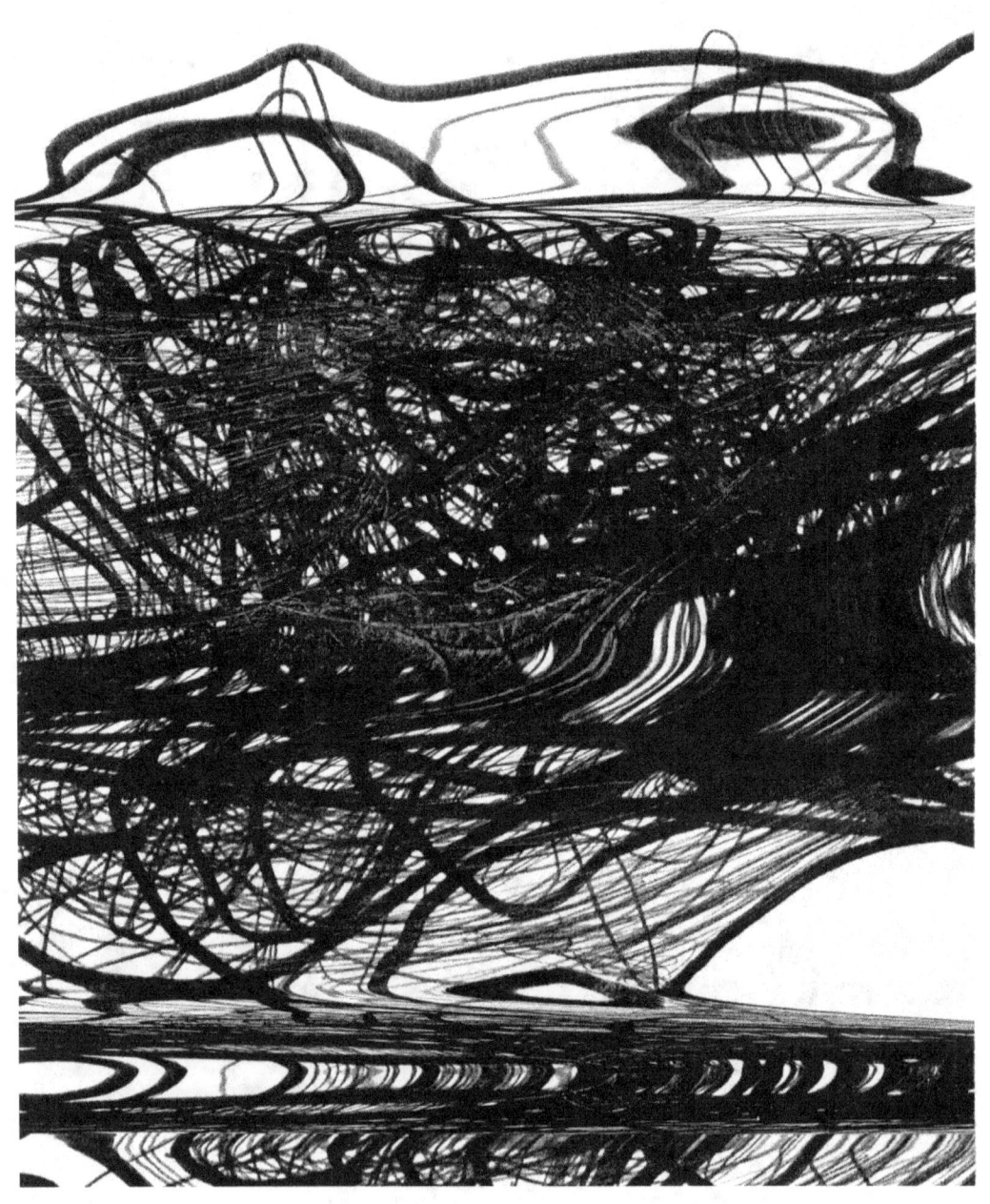

DIM DEMON

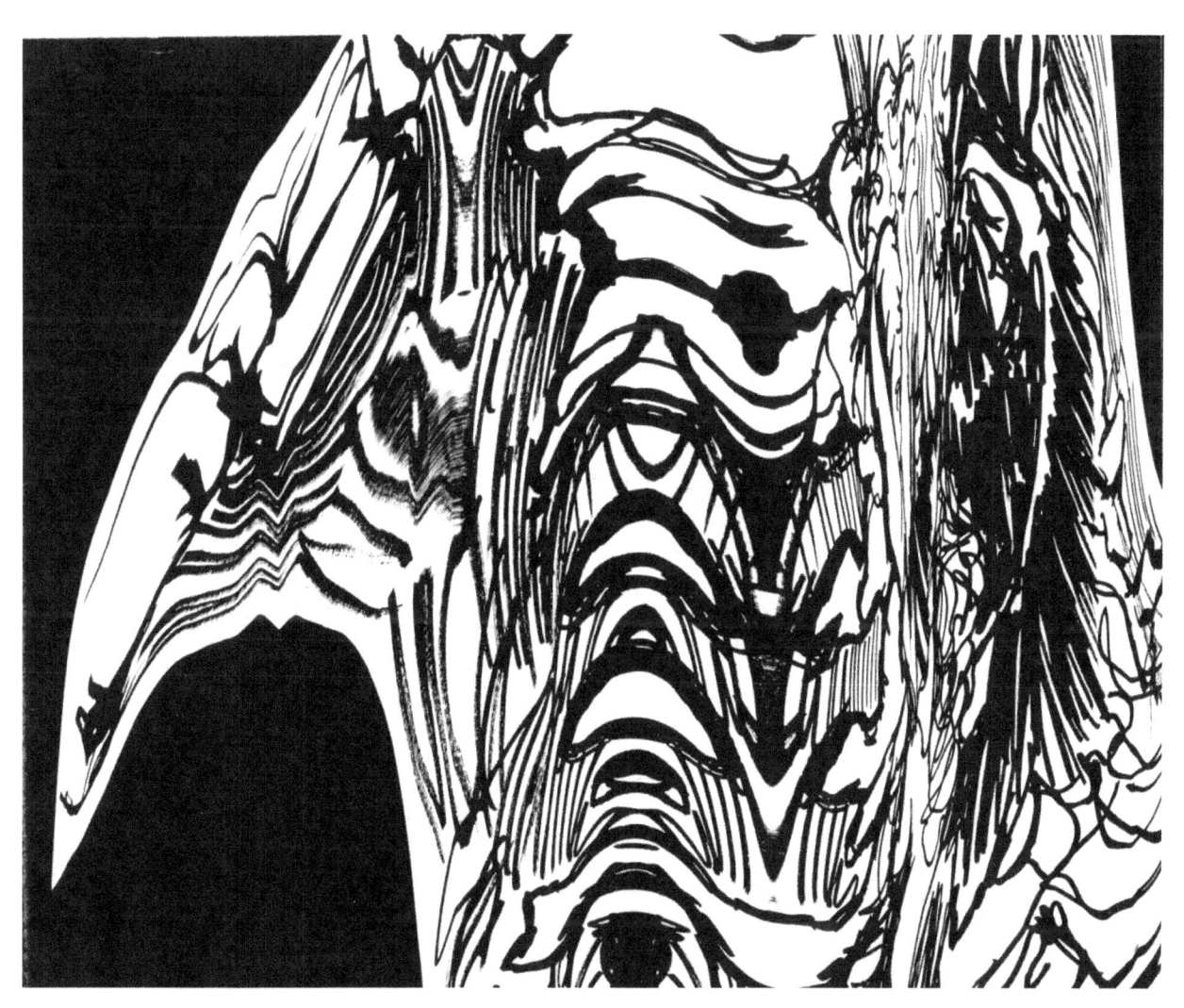

DINGBAT DEMON

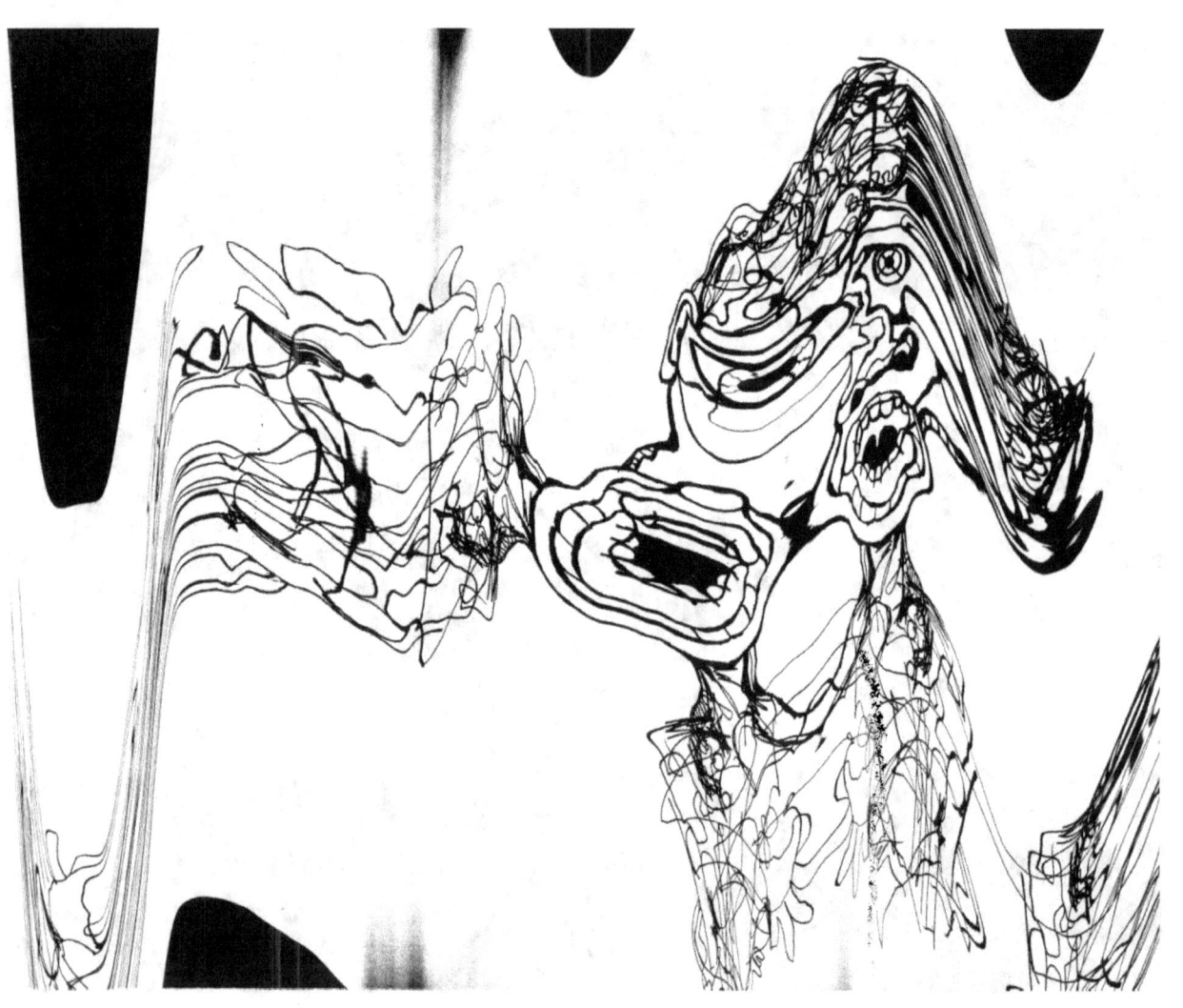

DIPHTHERIA DEMON

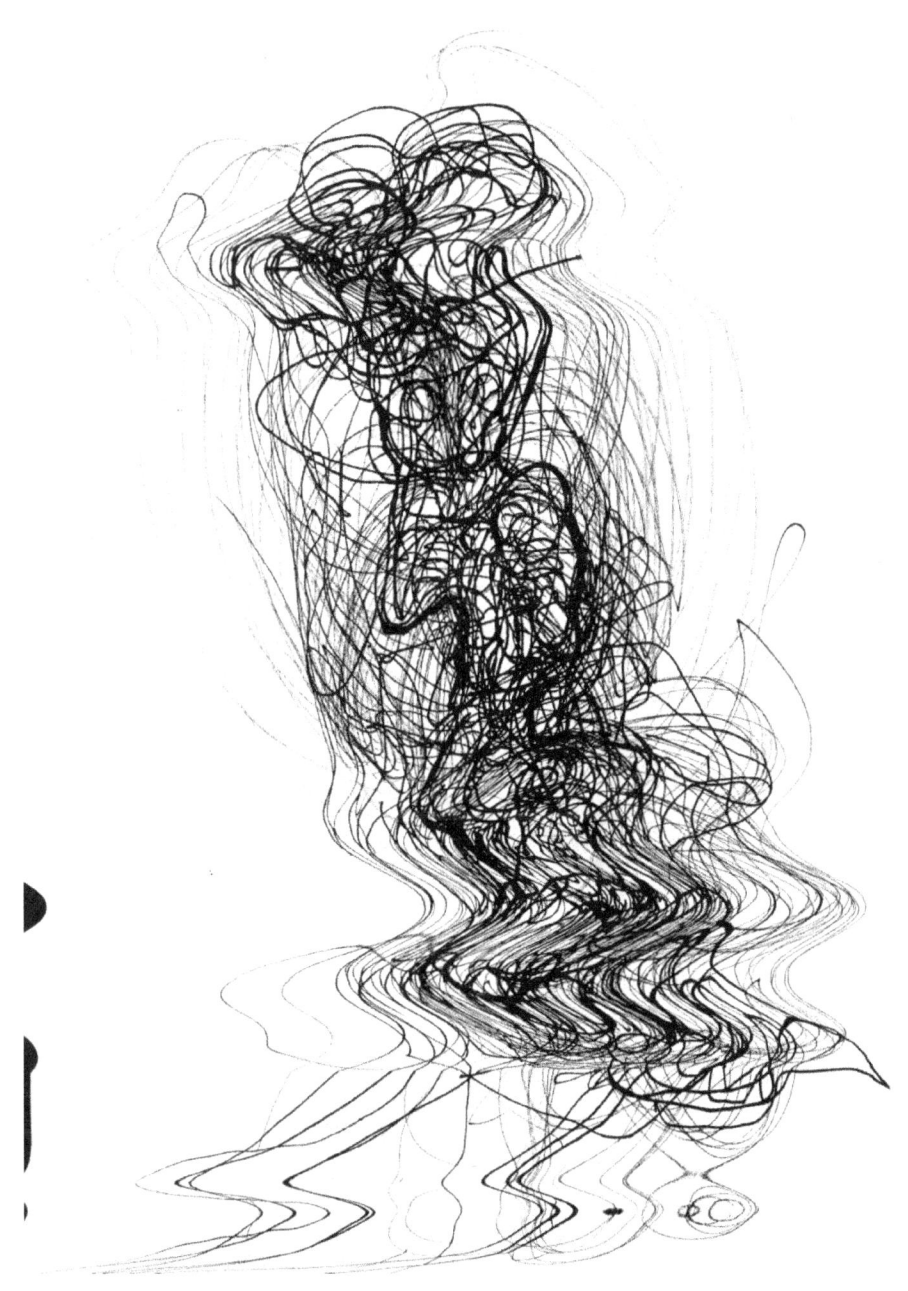

DIRTY LOOK DEMON

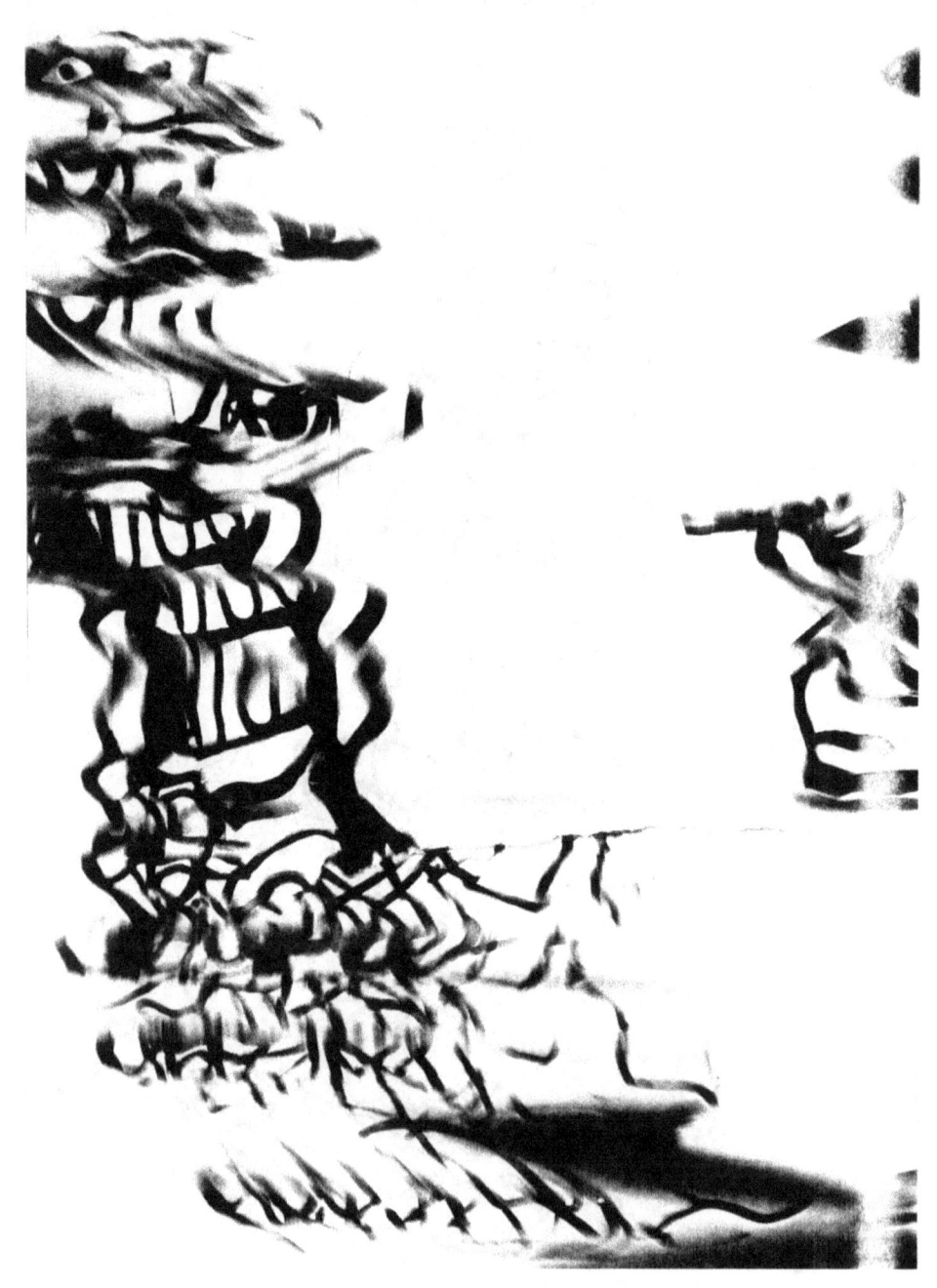

DISABLED DEMON

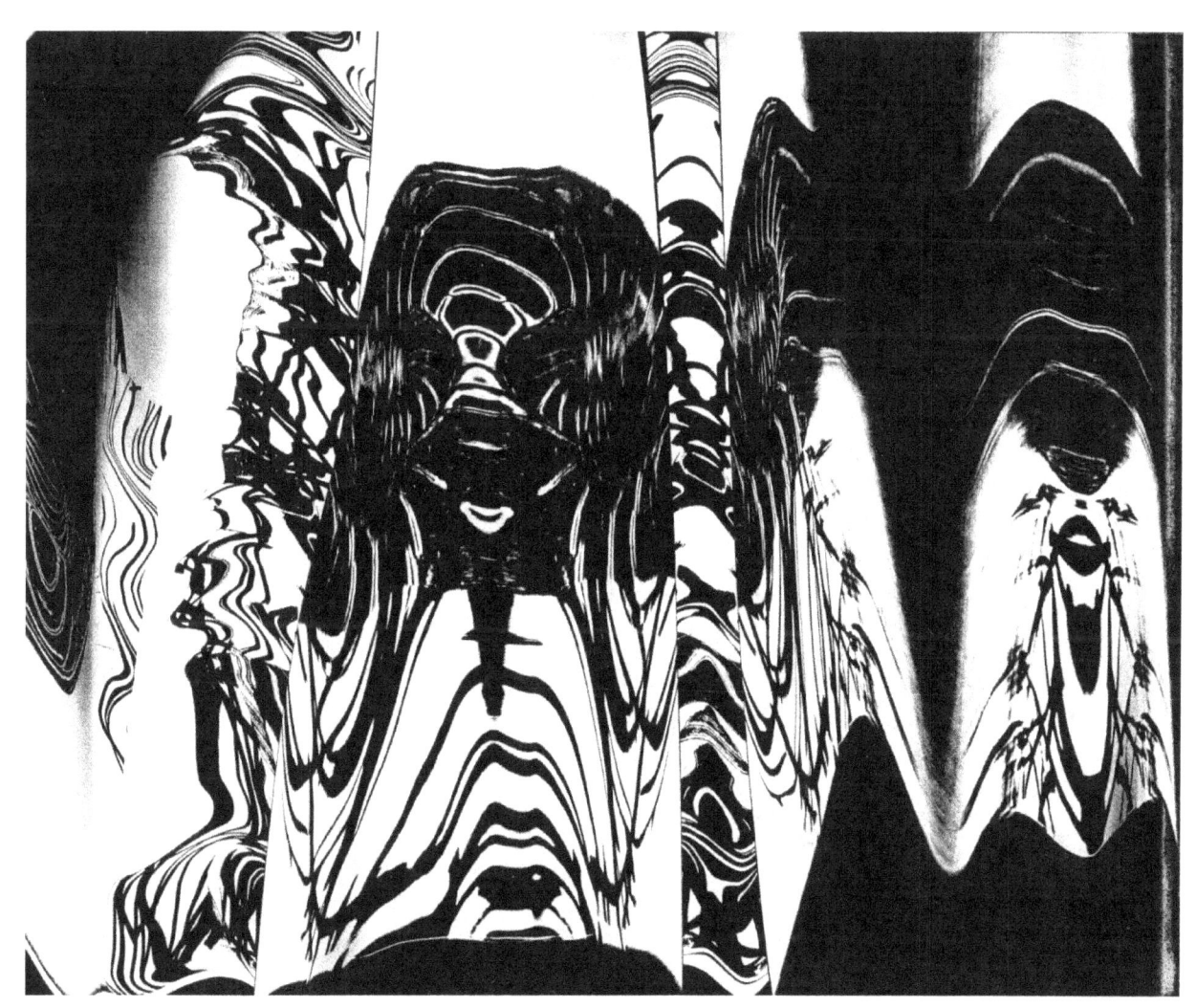

DISCIPLE DEMON

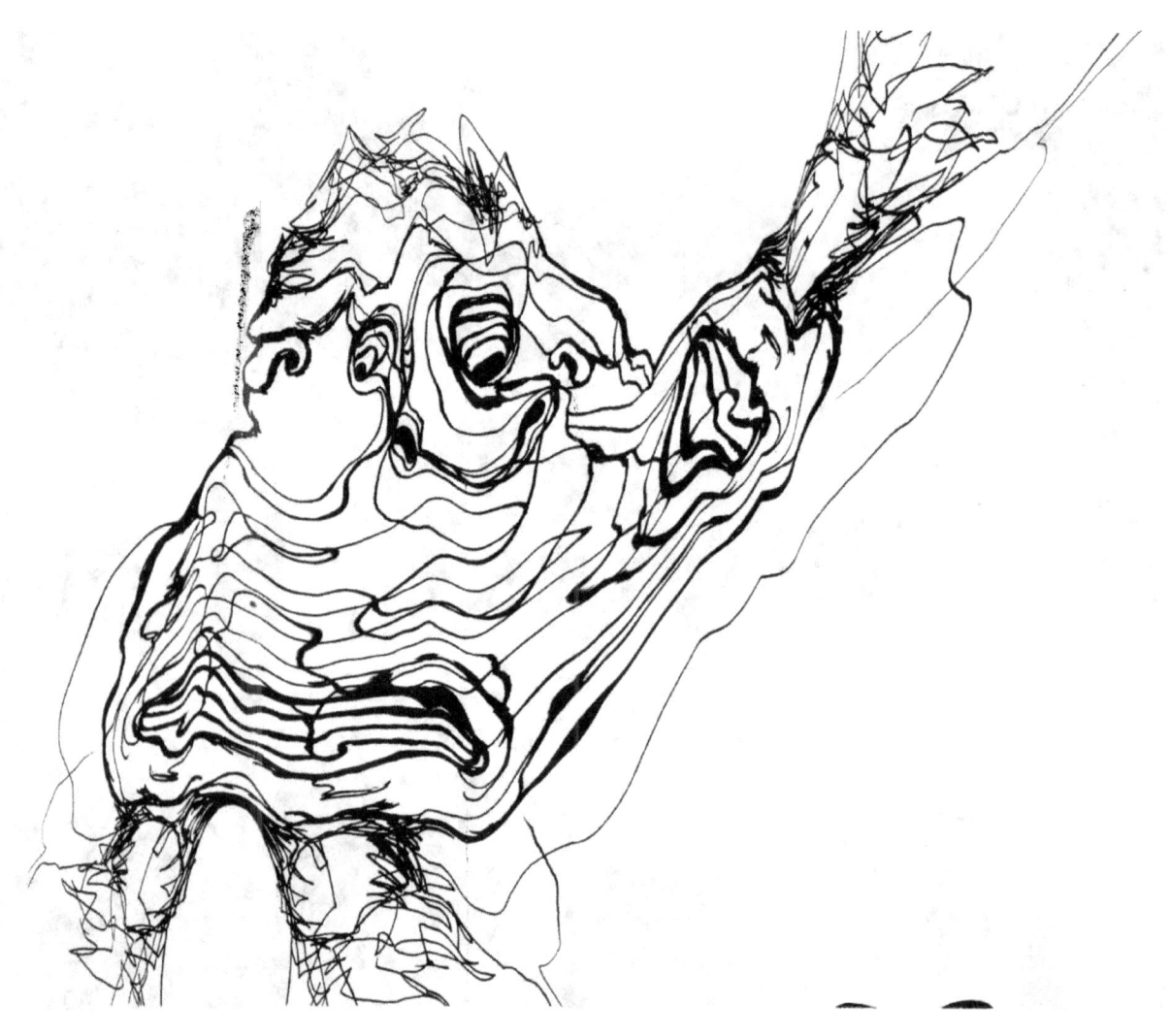

DISCURSIVE DEMON

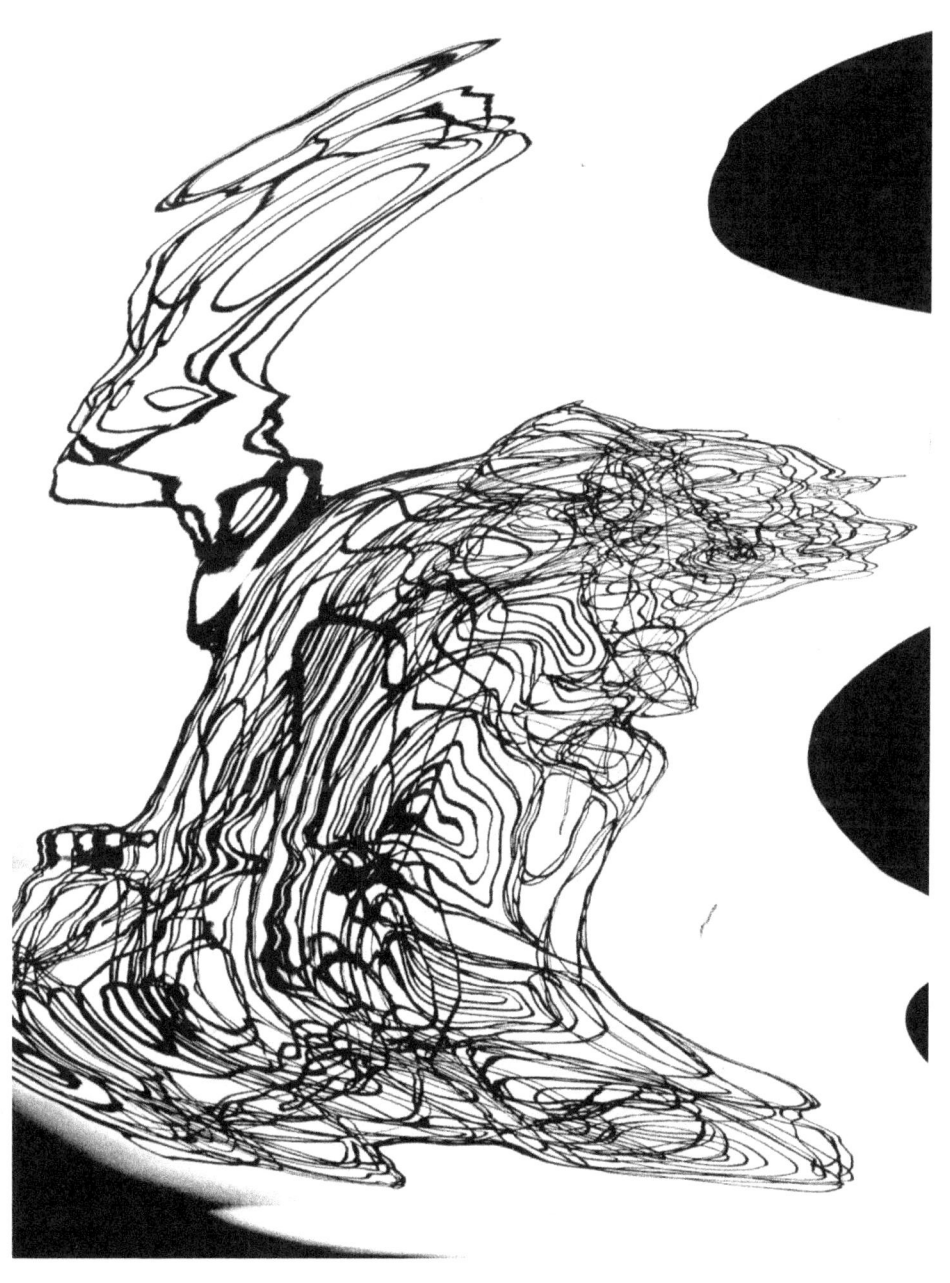

DISH CLOTH DEMON

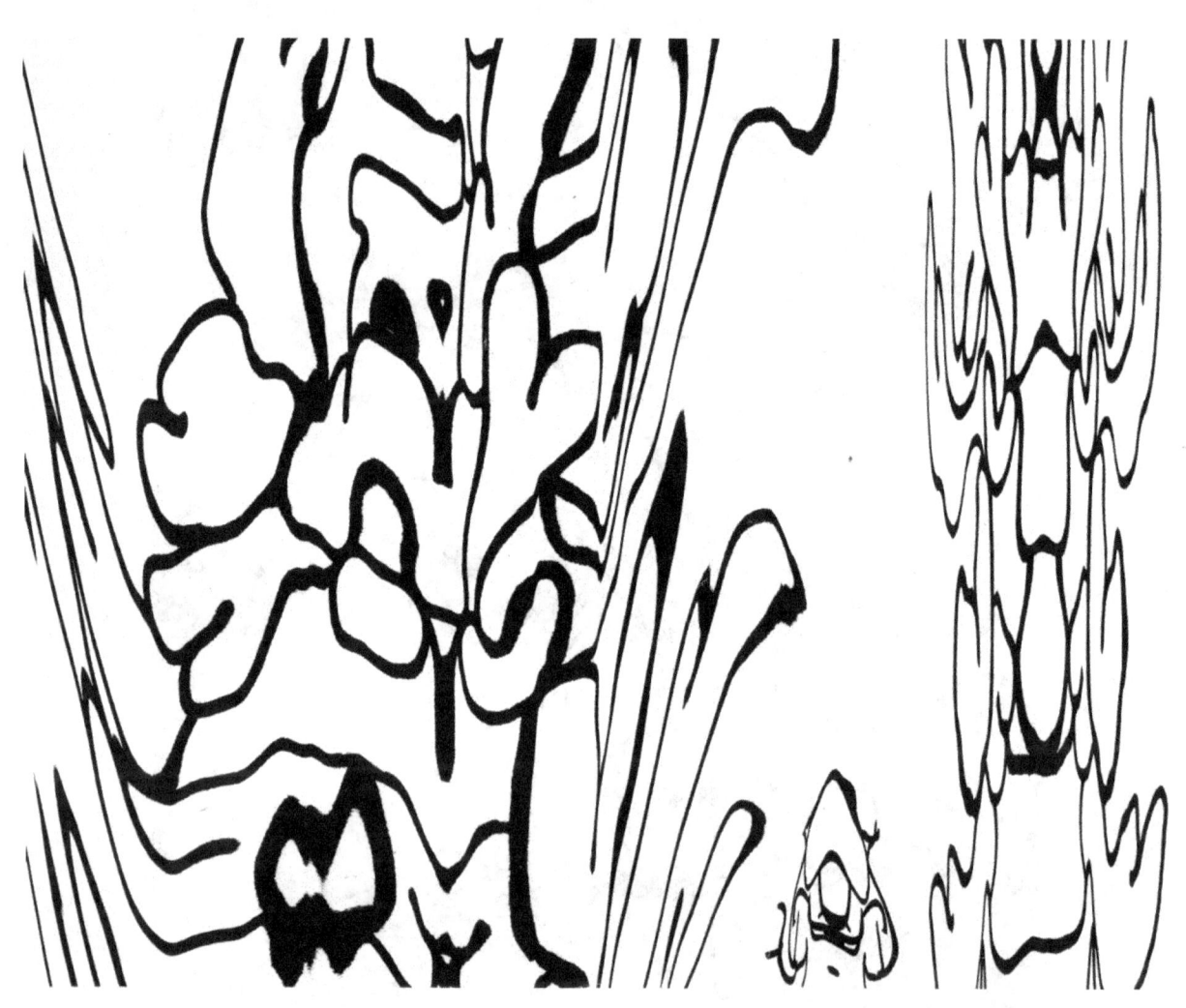

DISOBEYING DEMON

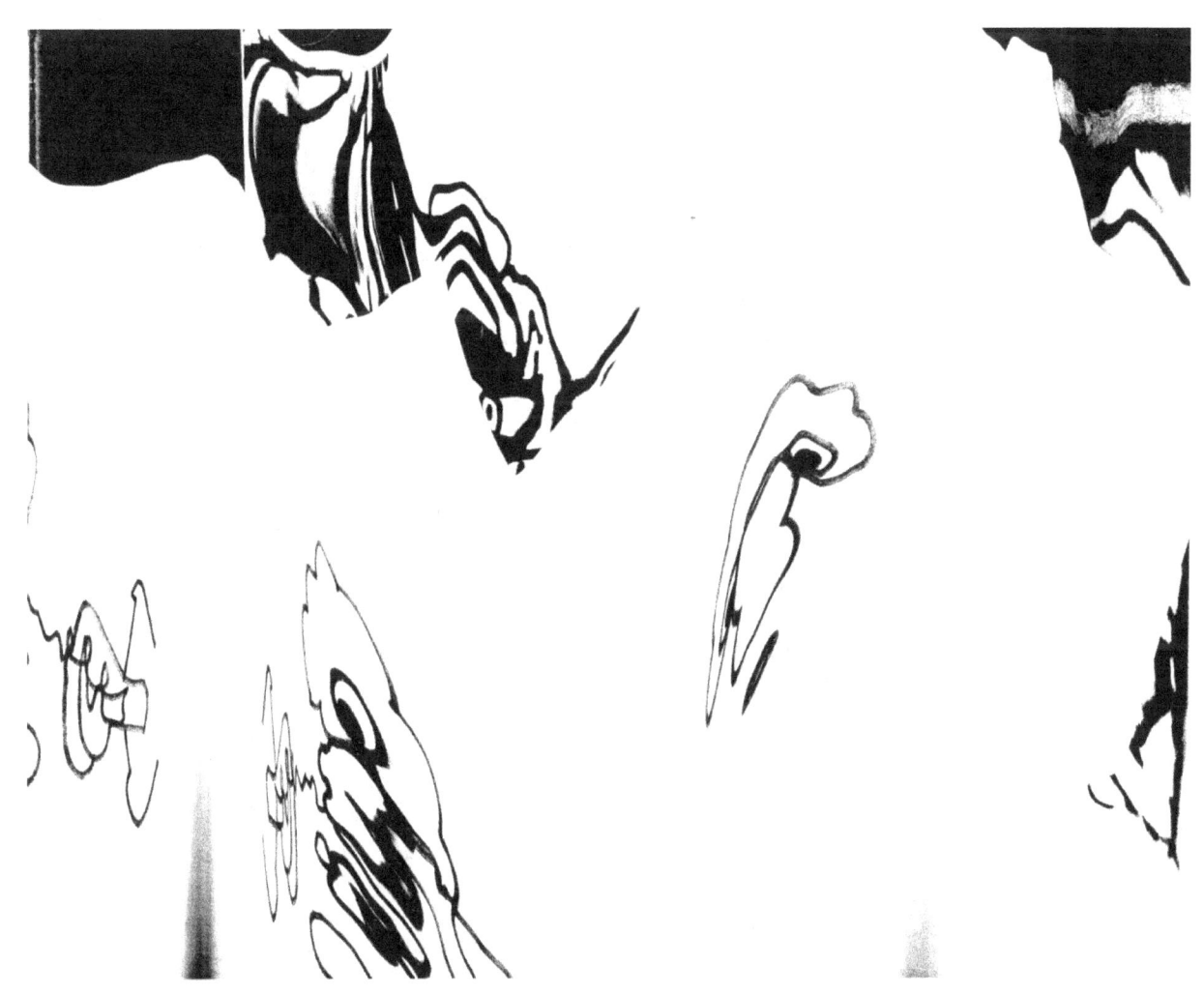

DIVINE DEMON

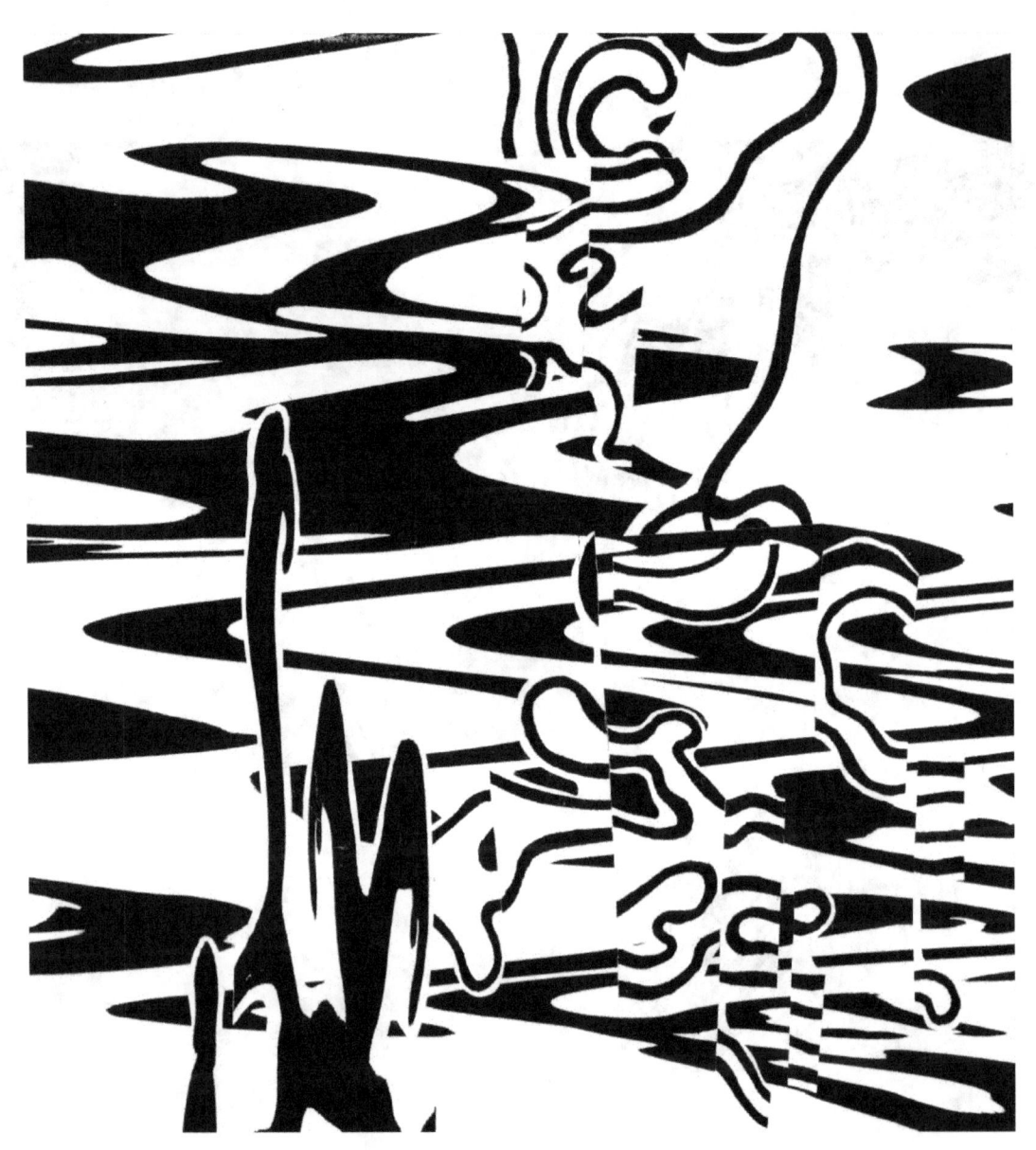

DNA DEMON

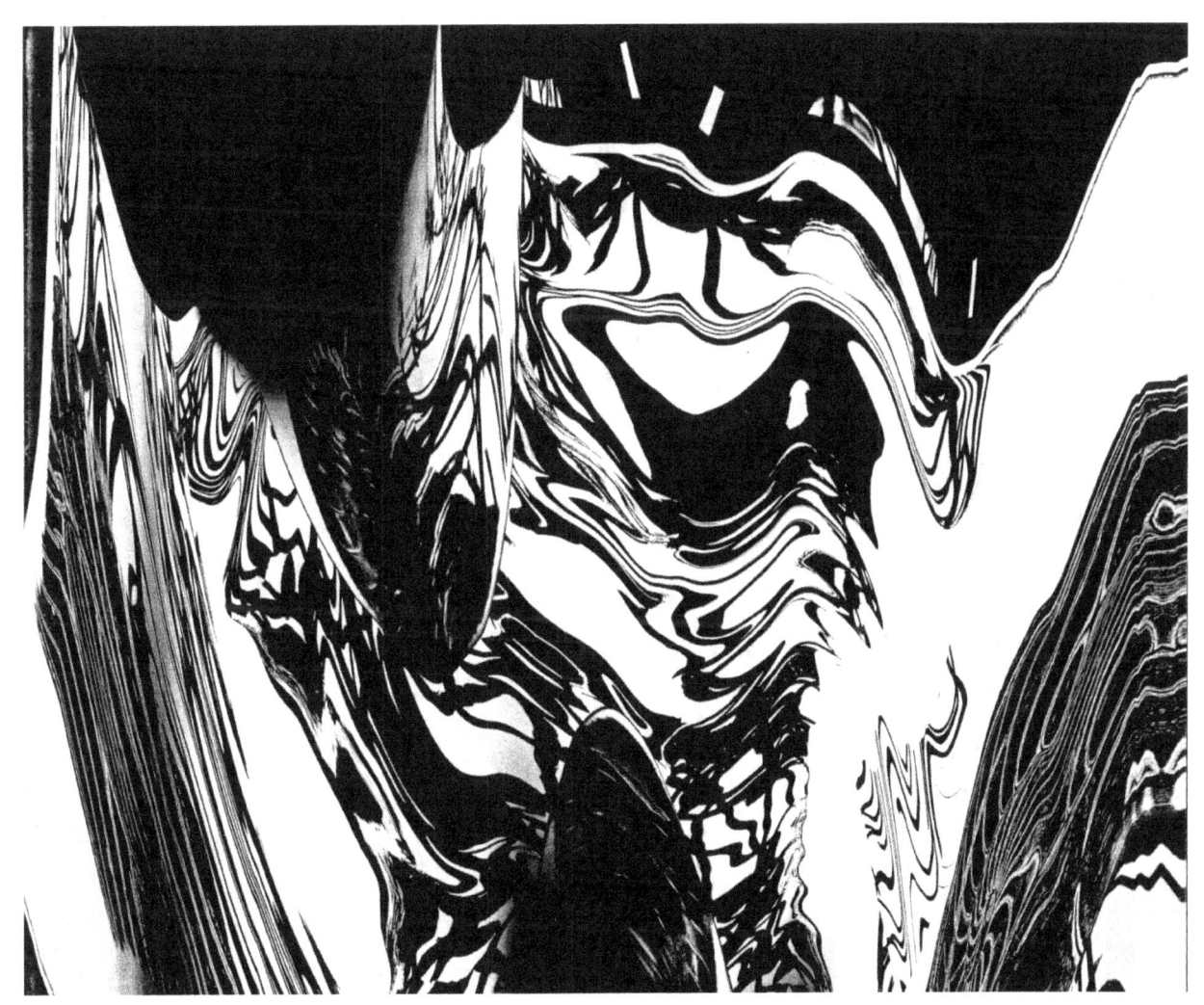

DOG LEG DEMON

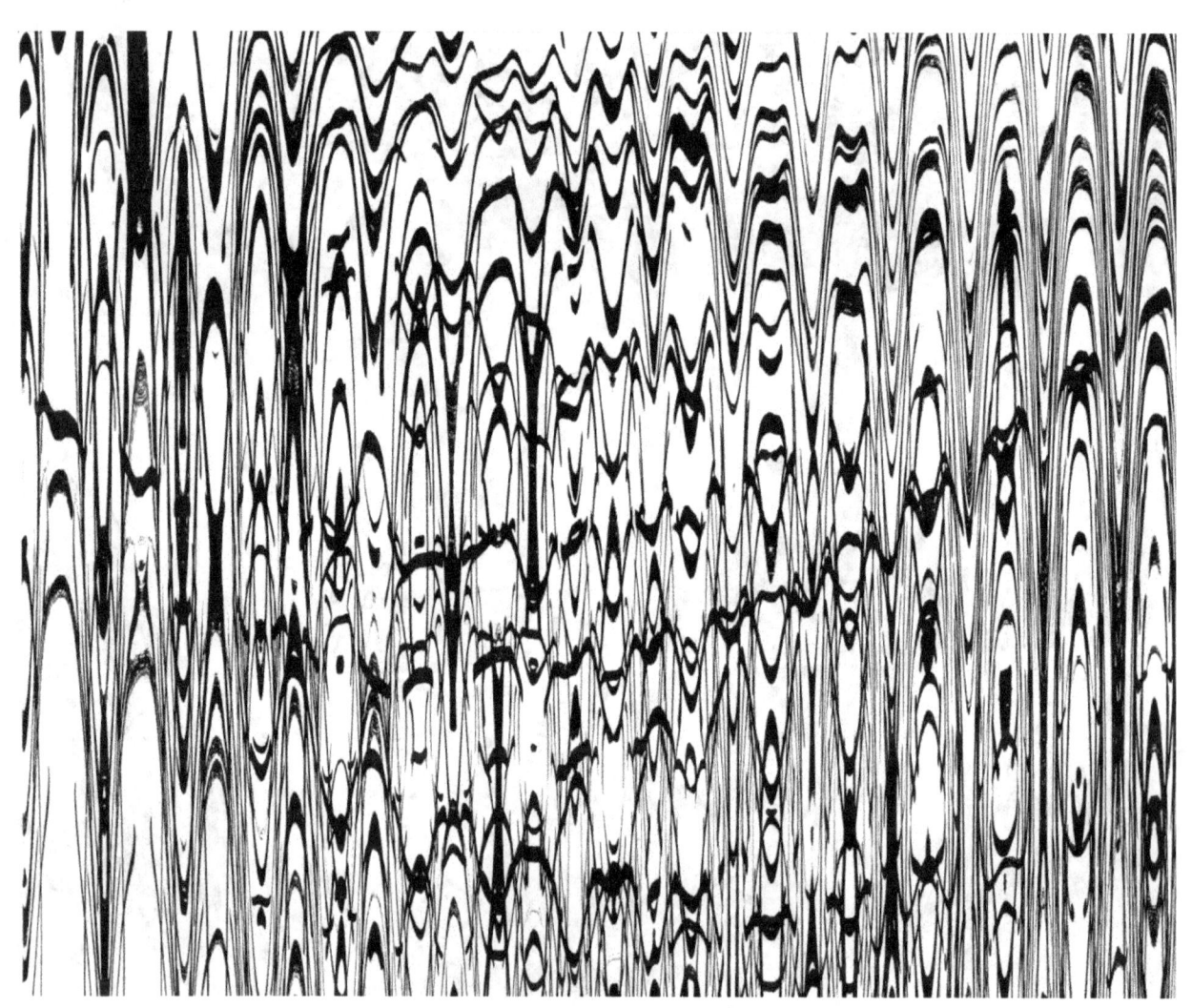

DOORBELL DEMON

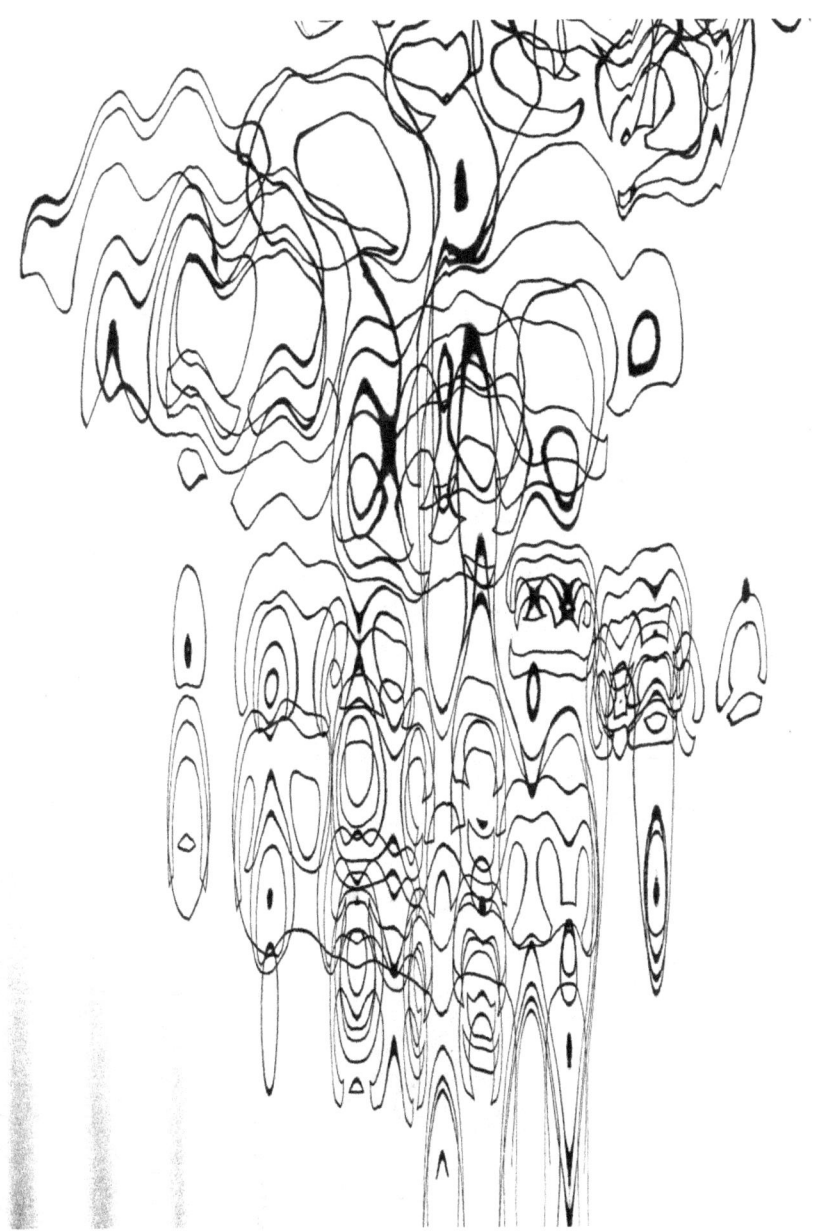

DOPE DEMON

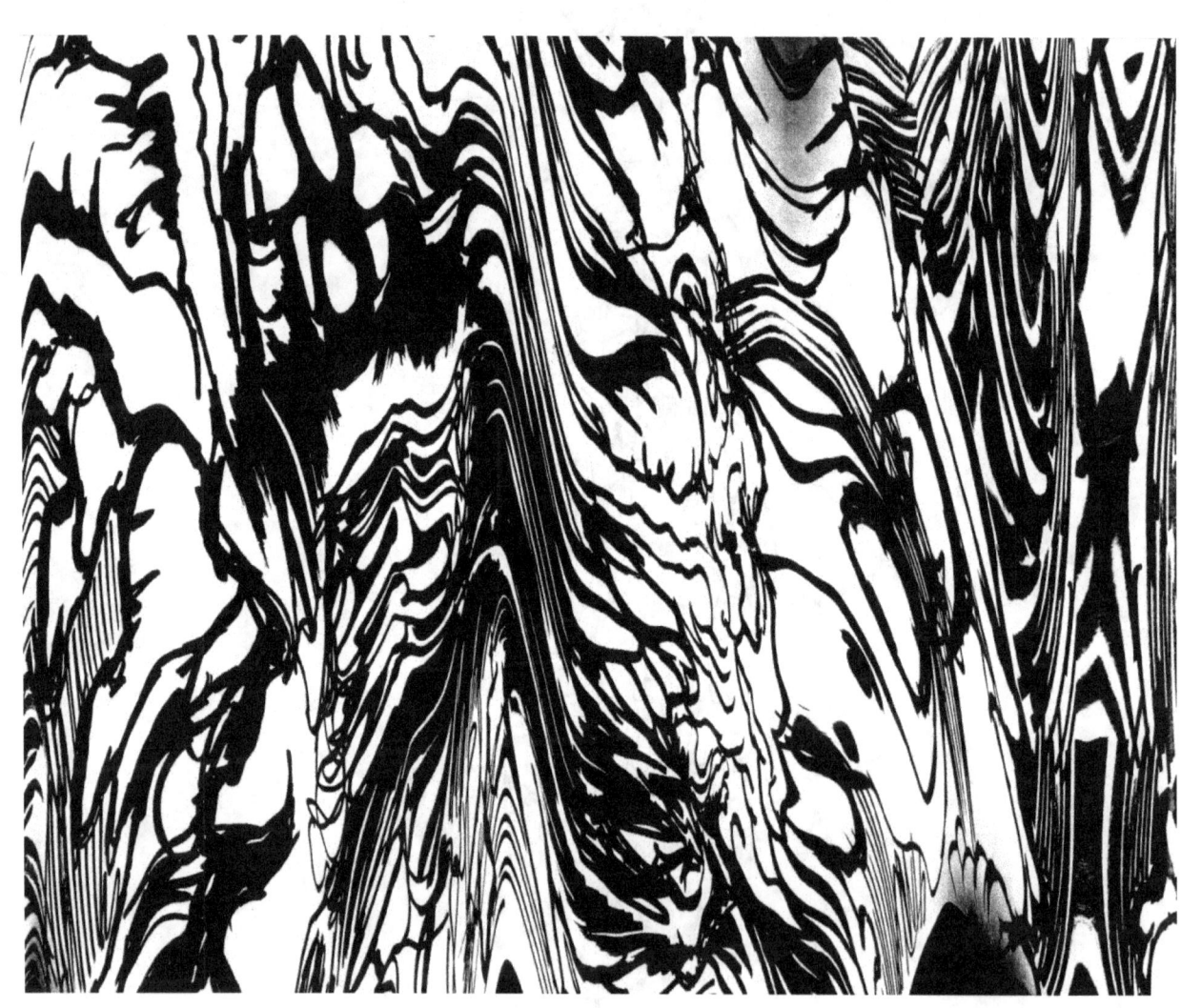

DURATION LANDSCAPE

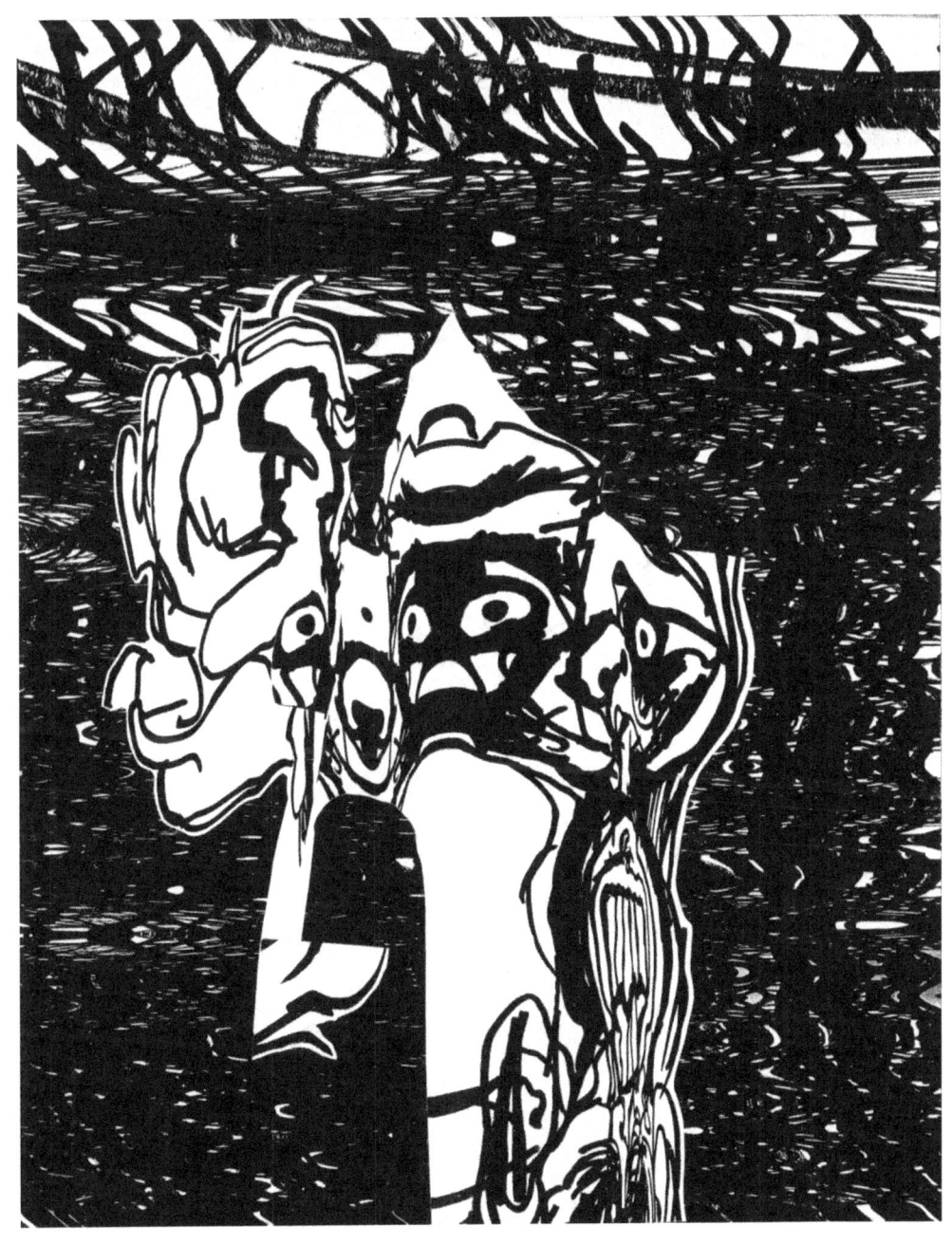

ELEMENTAL

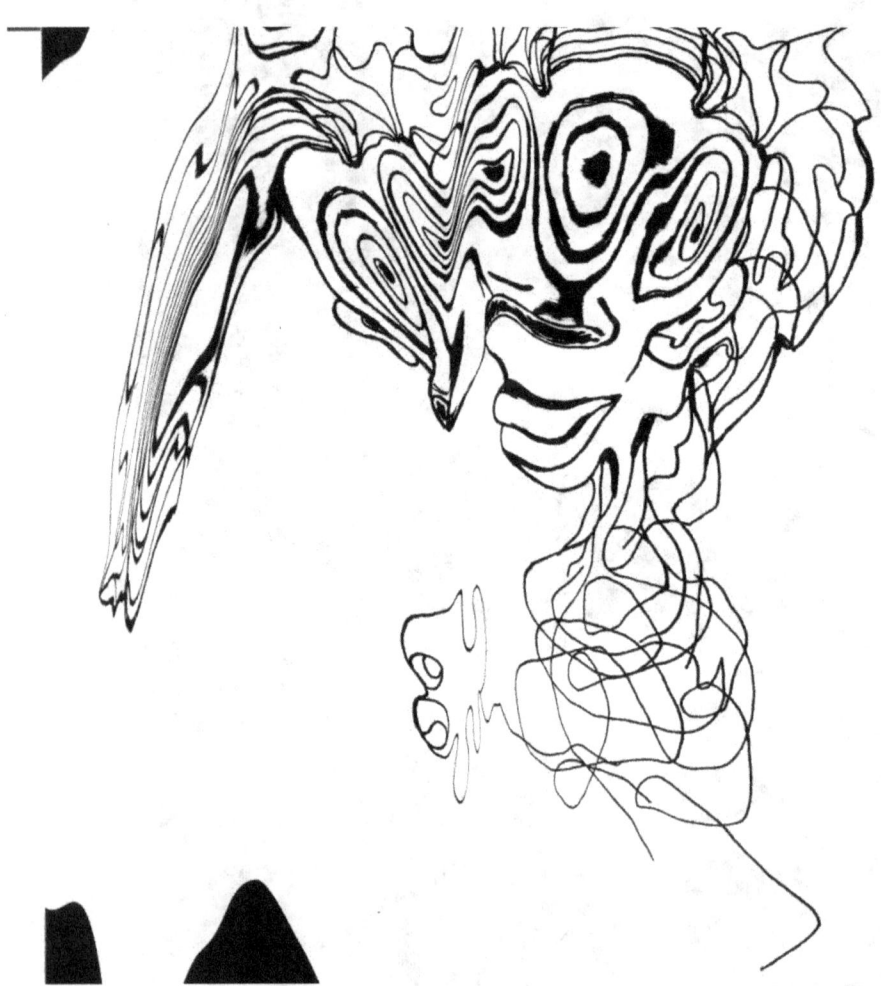

FIVE FLUIDS

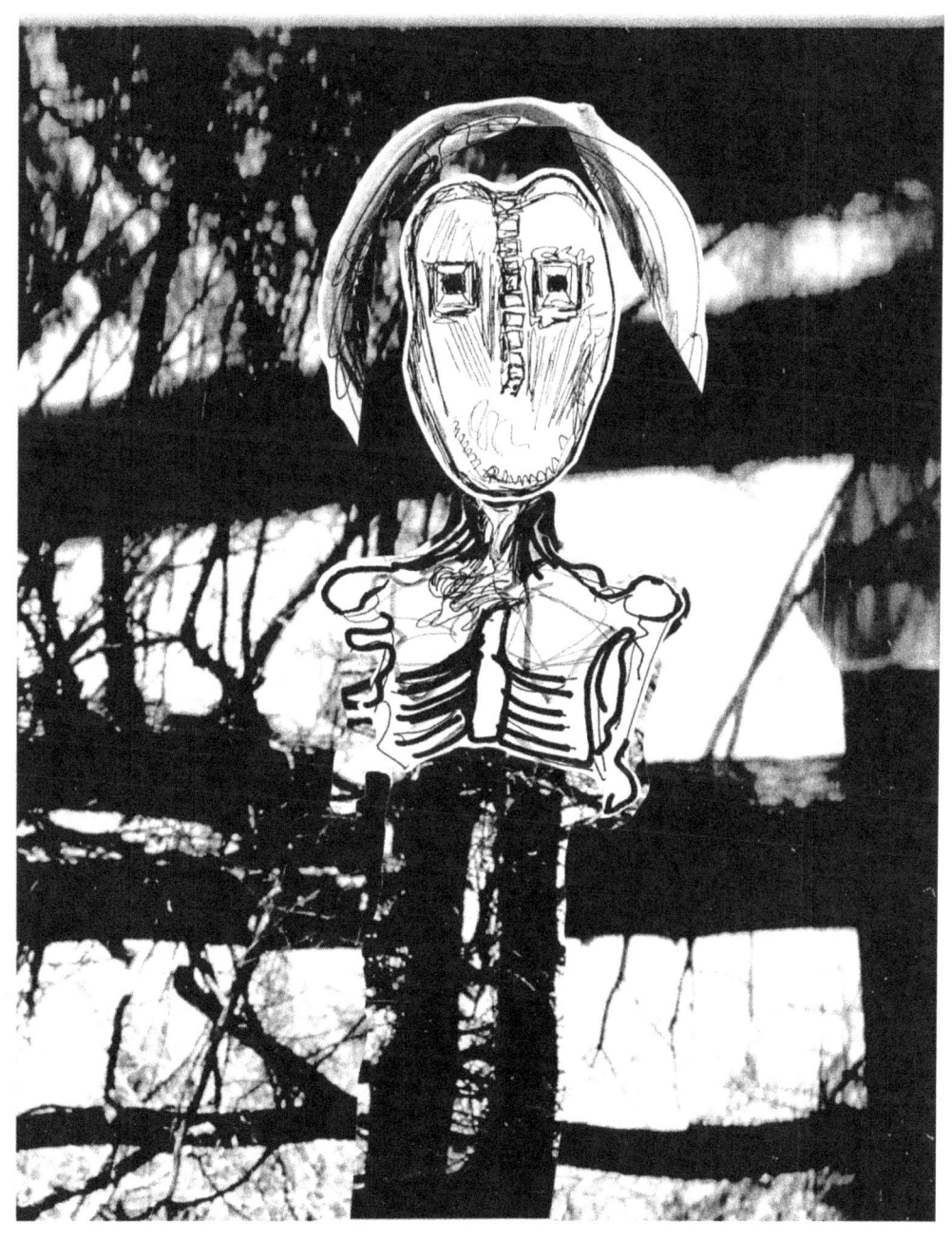

FOREST SORE

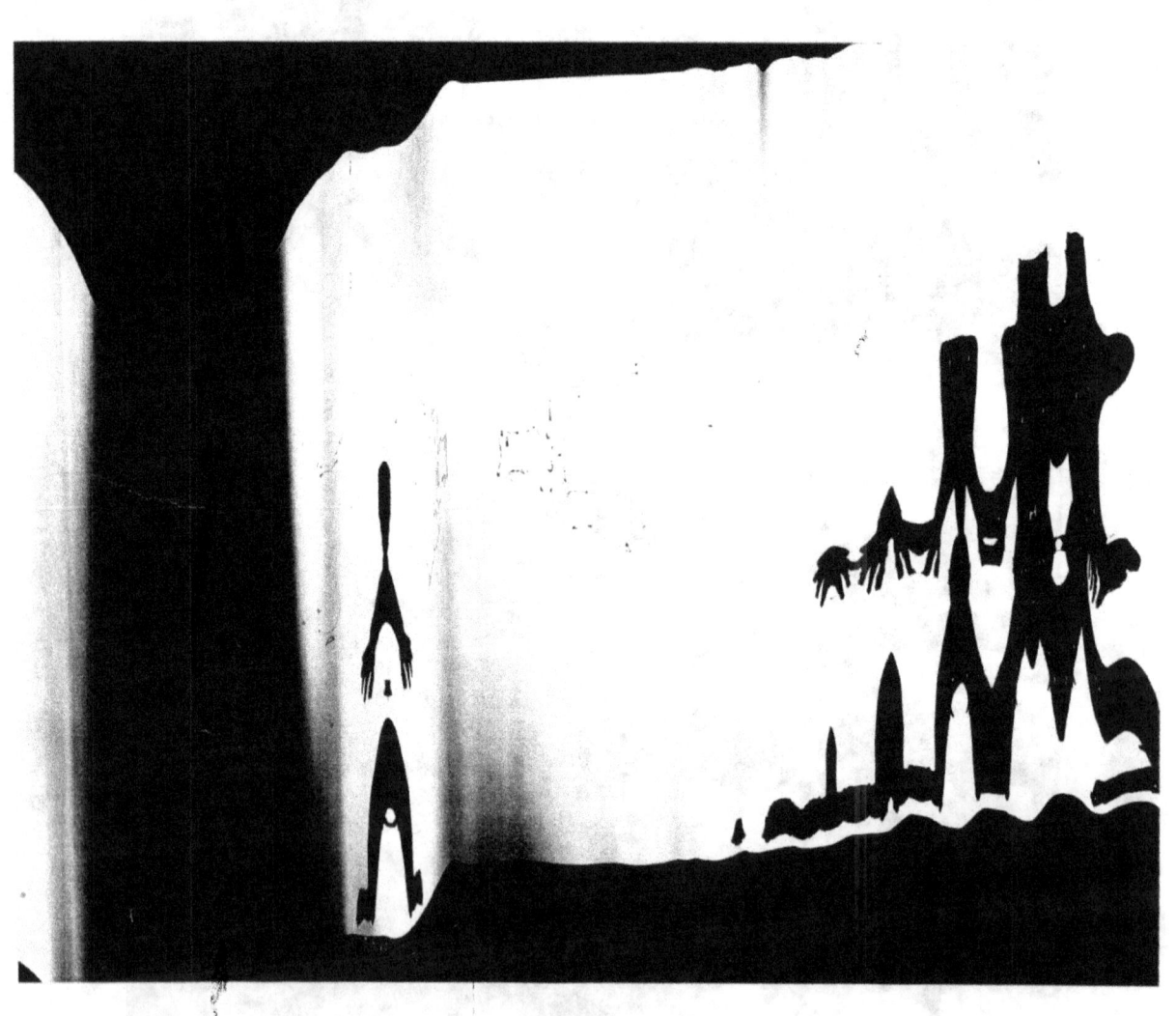

FUTURE SHADOWS

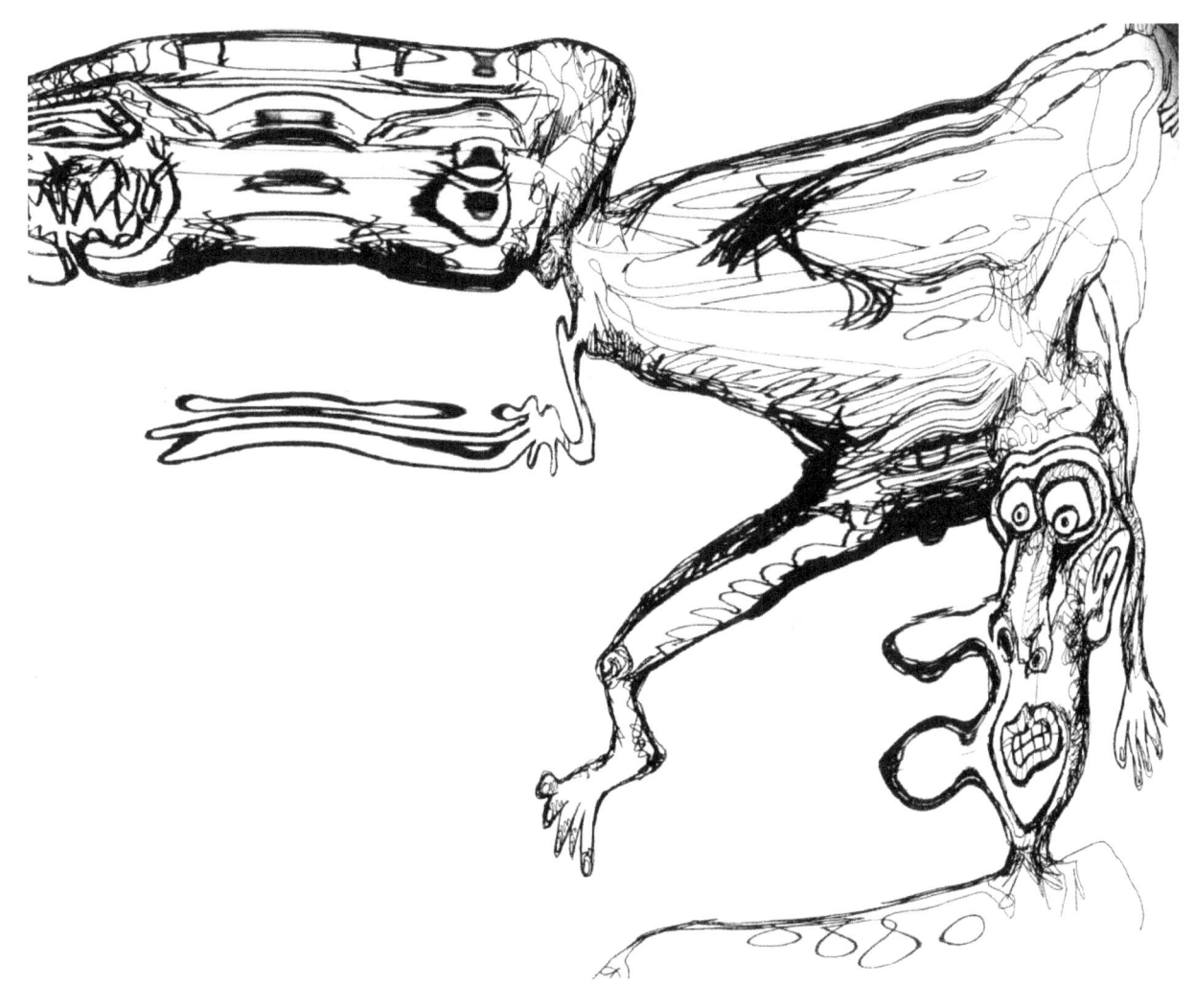

GOITER

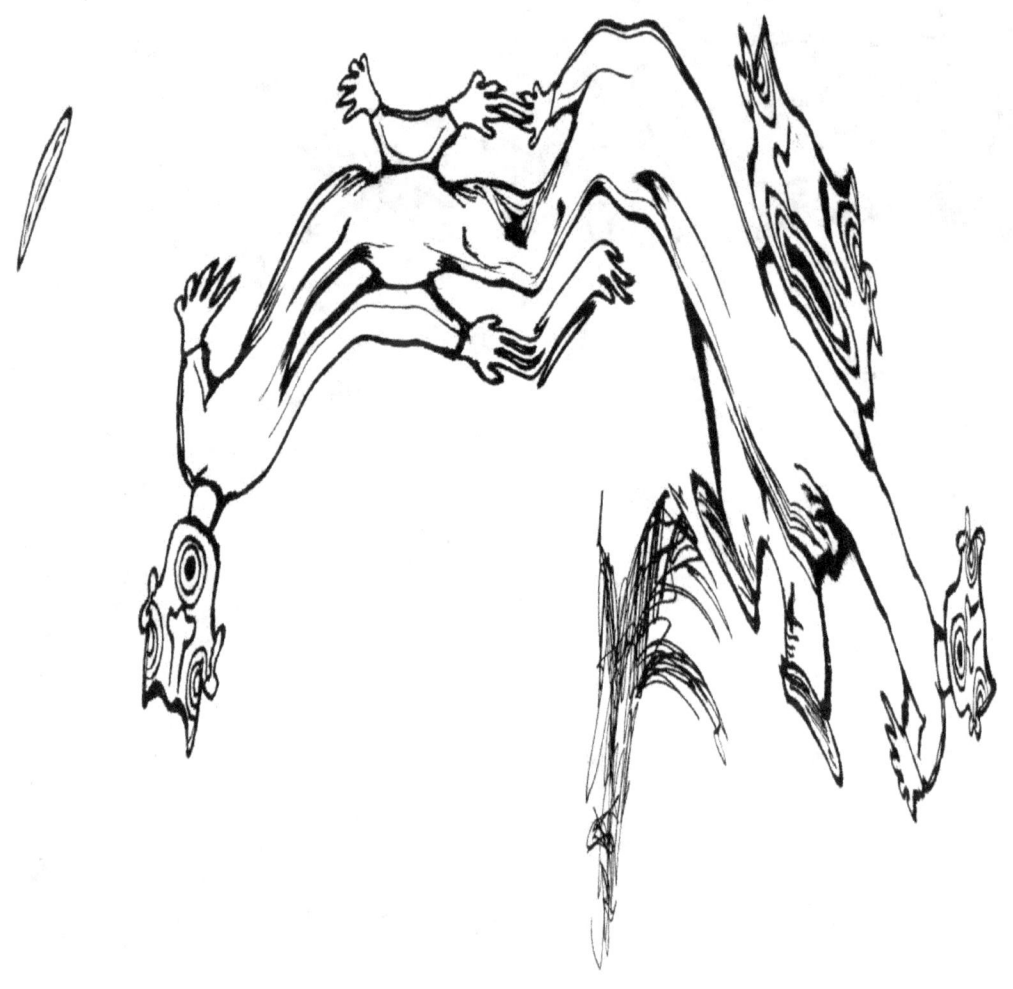

HANDS

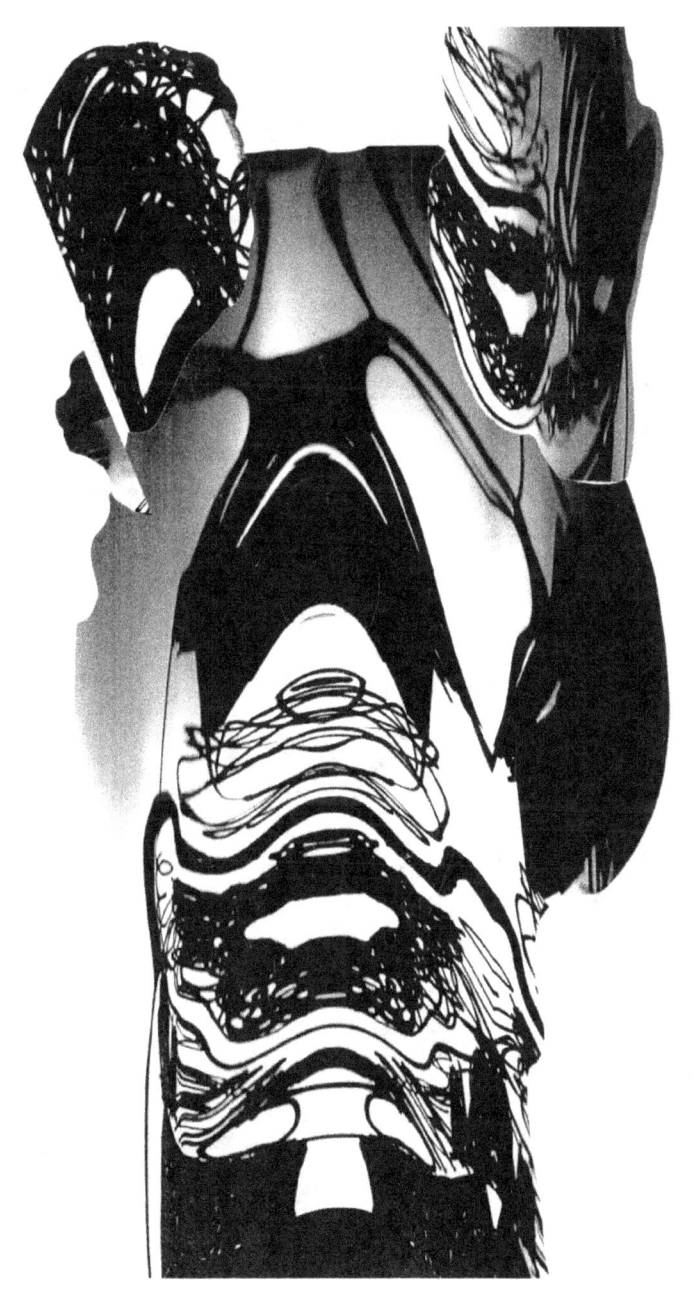

HELMET

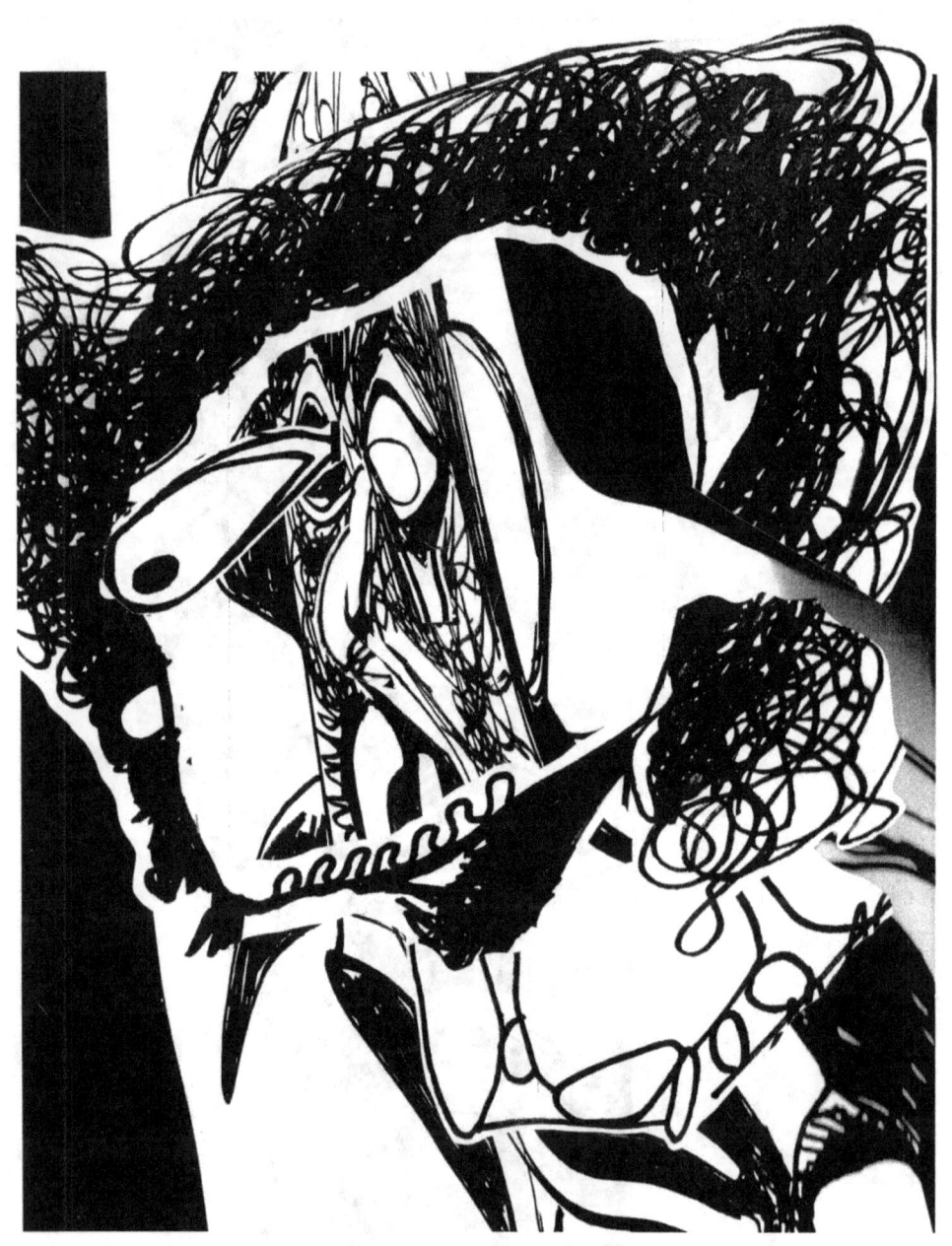

HOMOSEXUALS

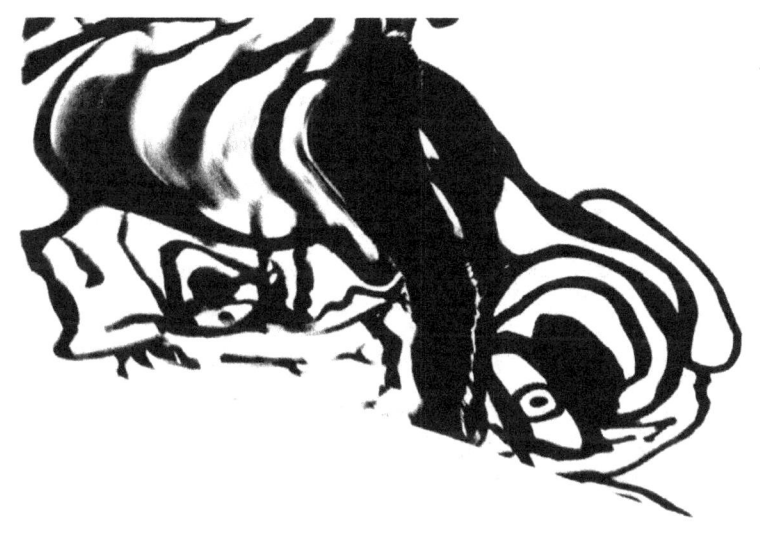

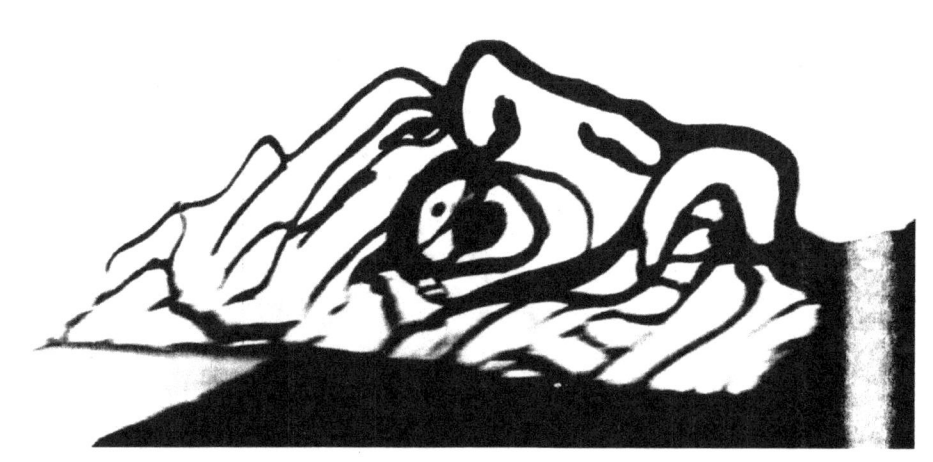

KAFKA PARKWAY

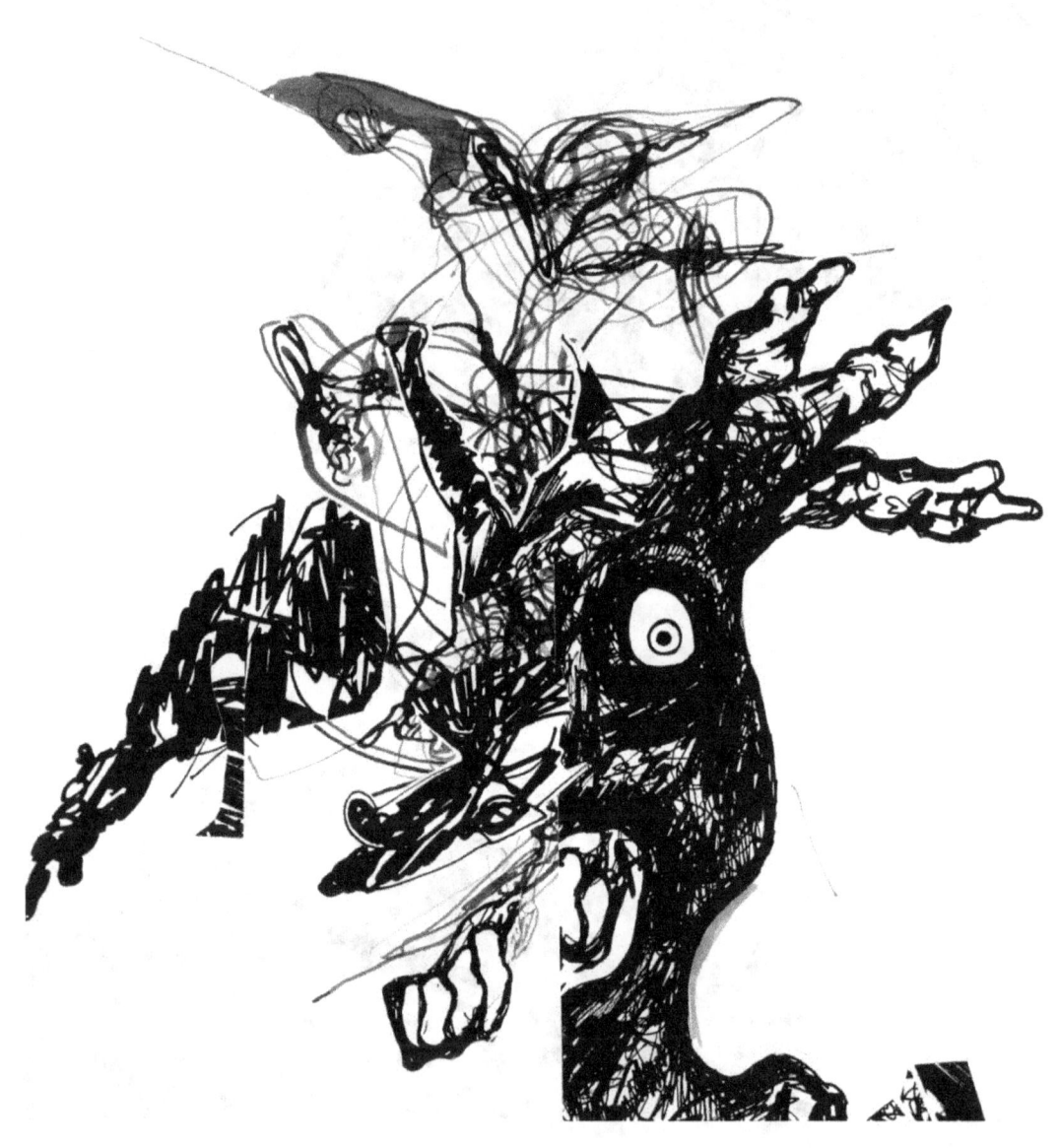

KNIFEMAN

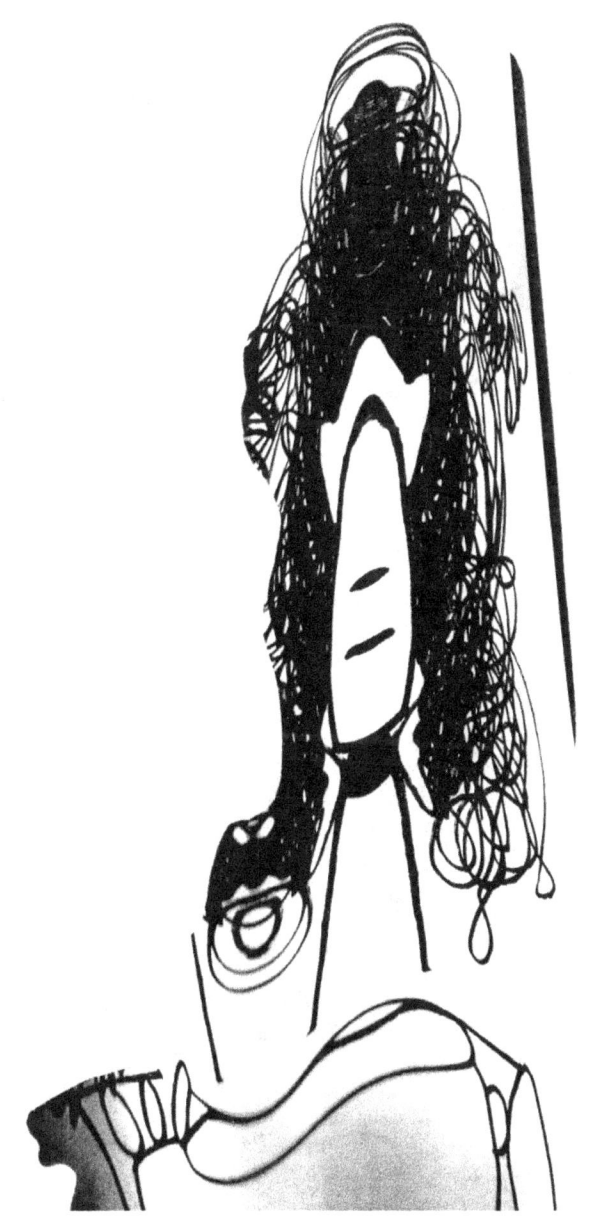

LIEGE

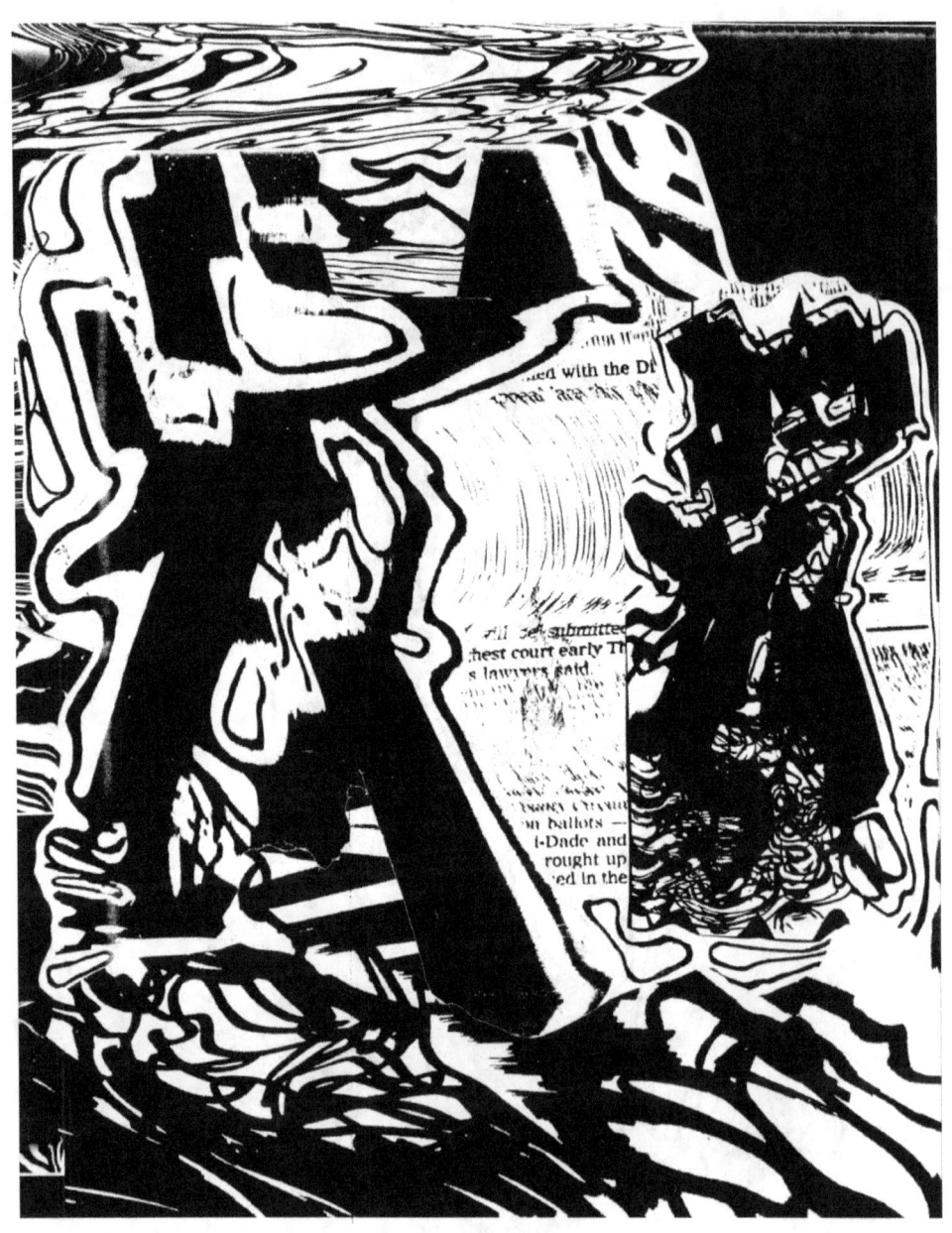

LOST GRACE

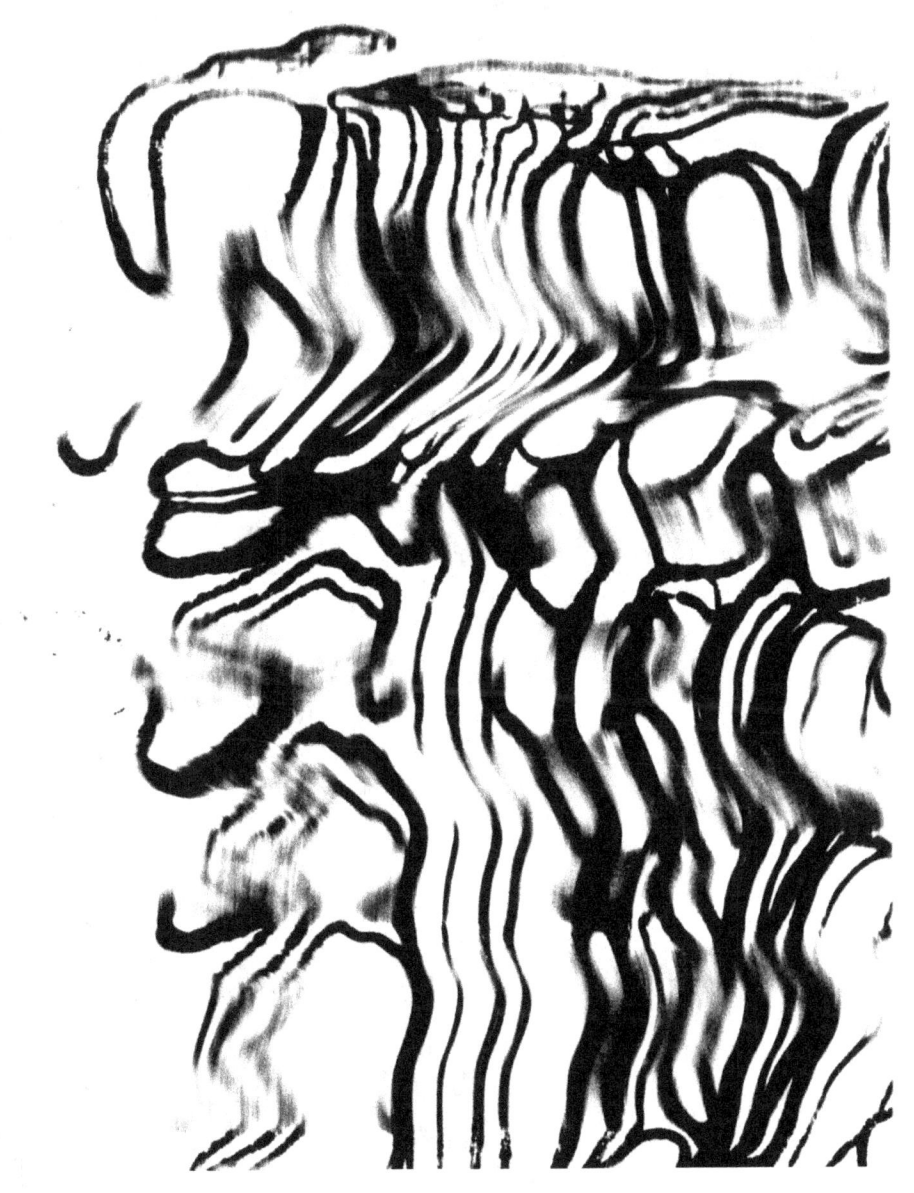

MOUND

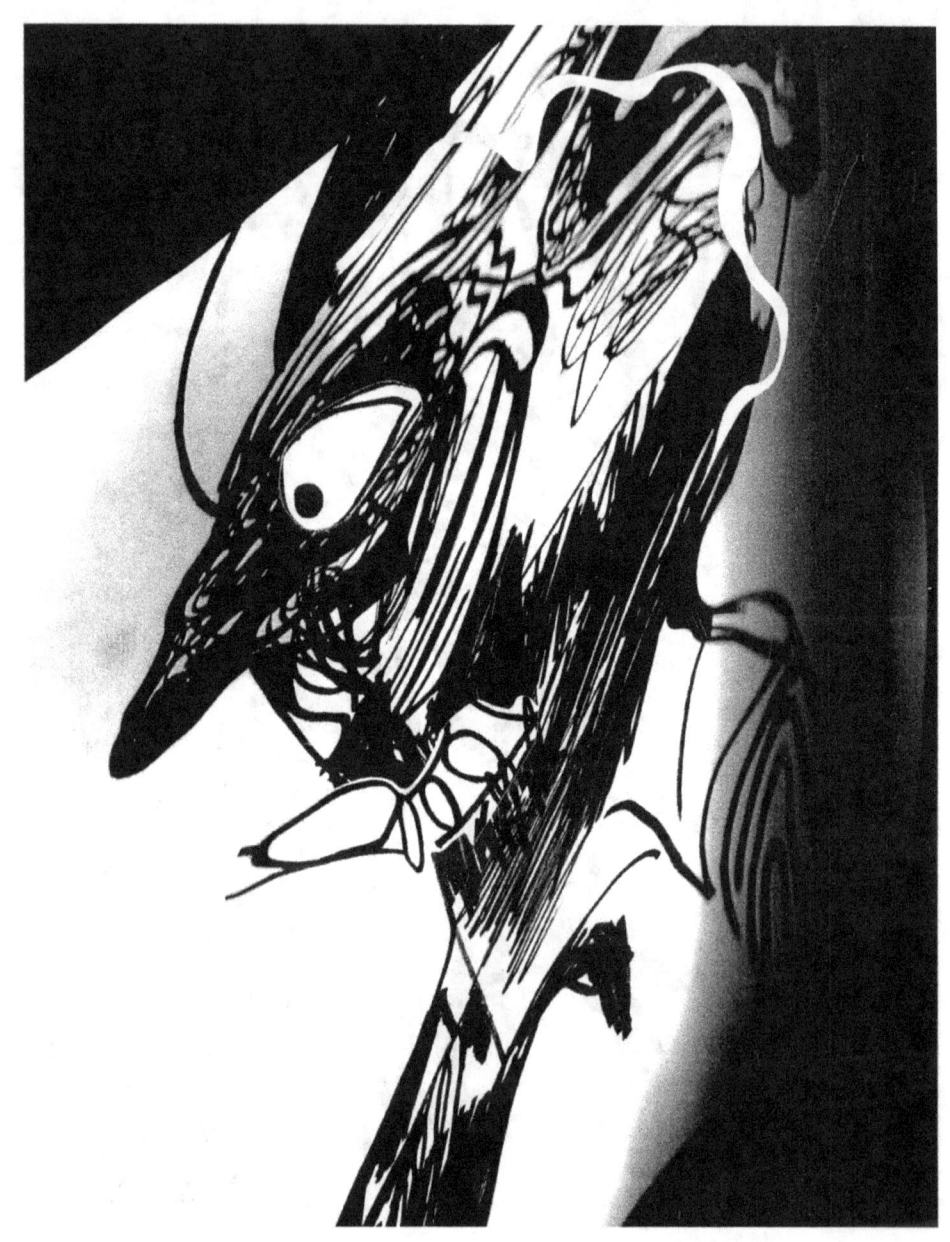

PAGAN

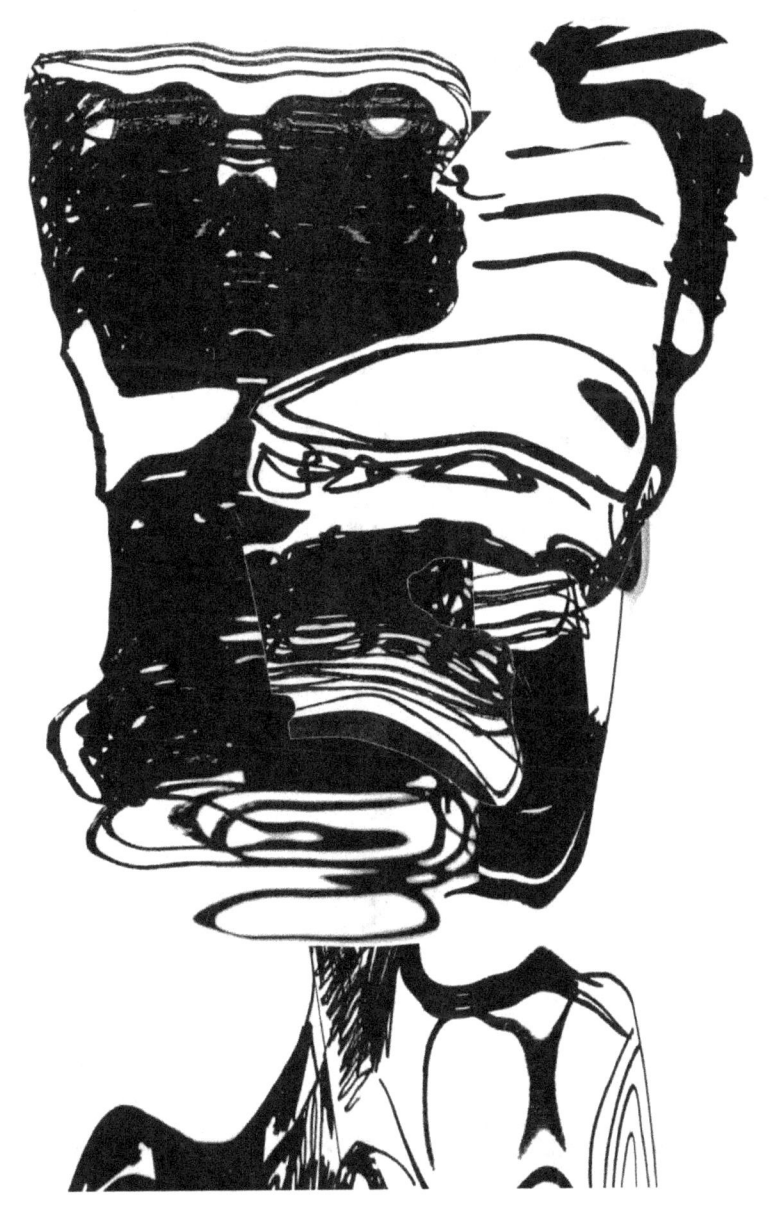

PANTYHOSE RESTARTER

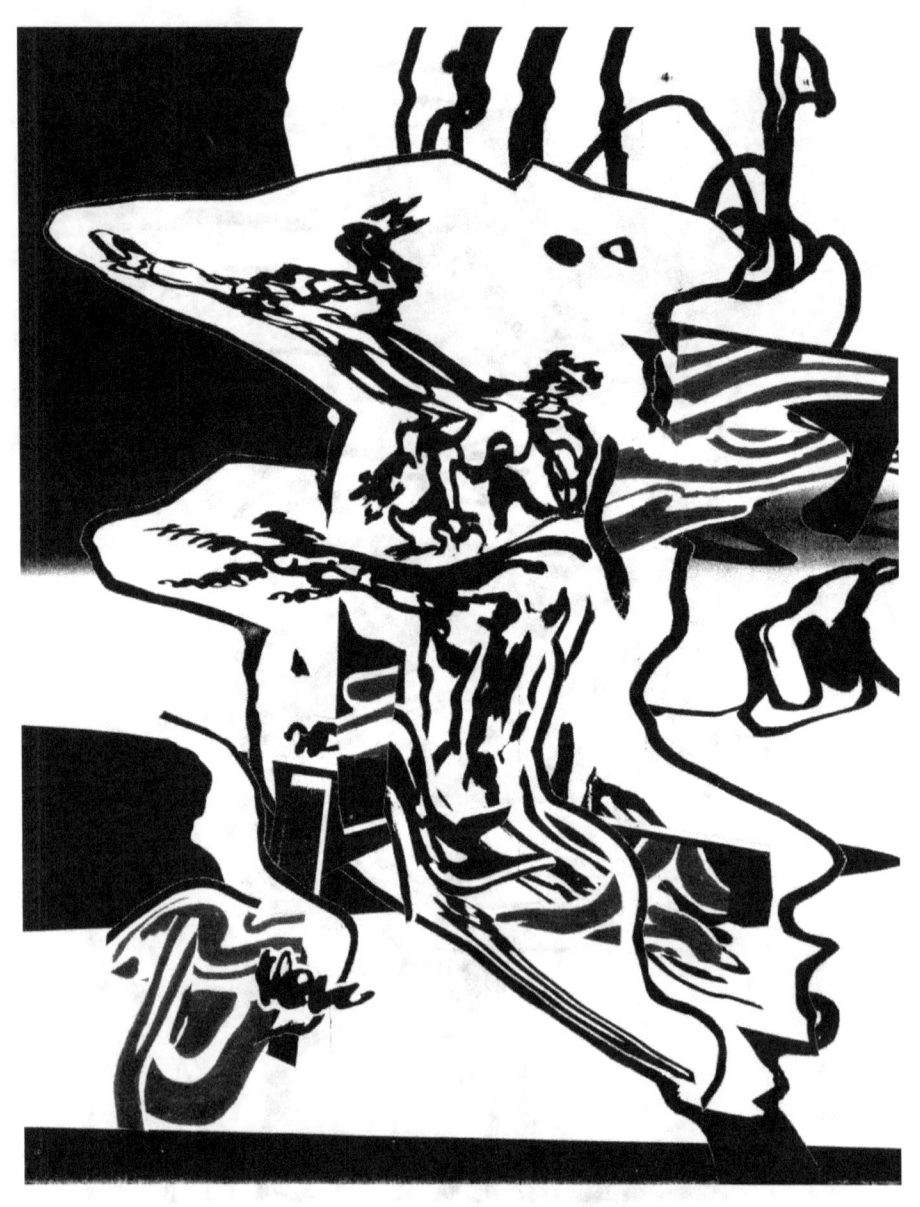

PERIMETER

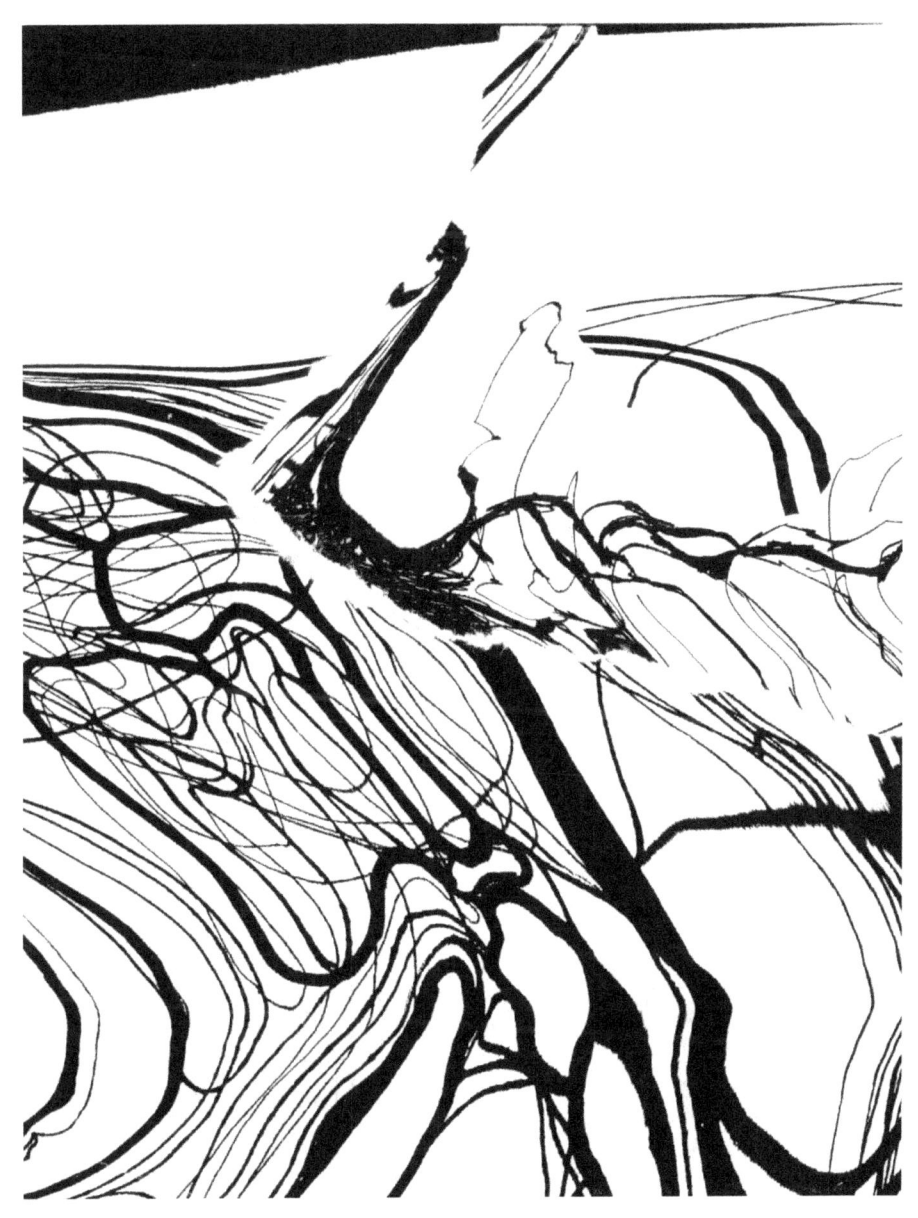

POINTY LAKE

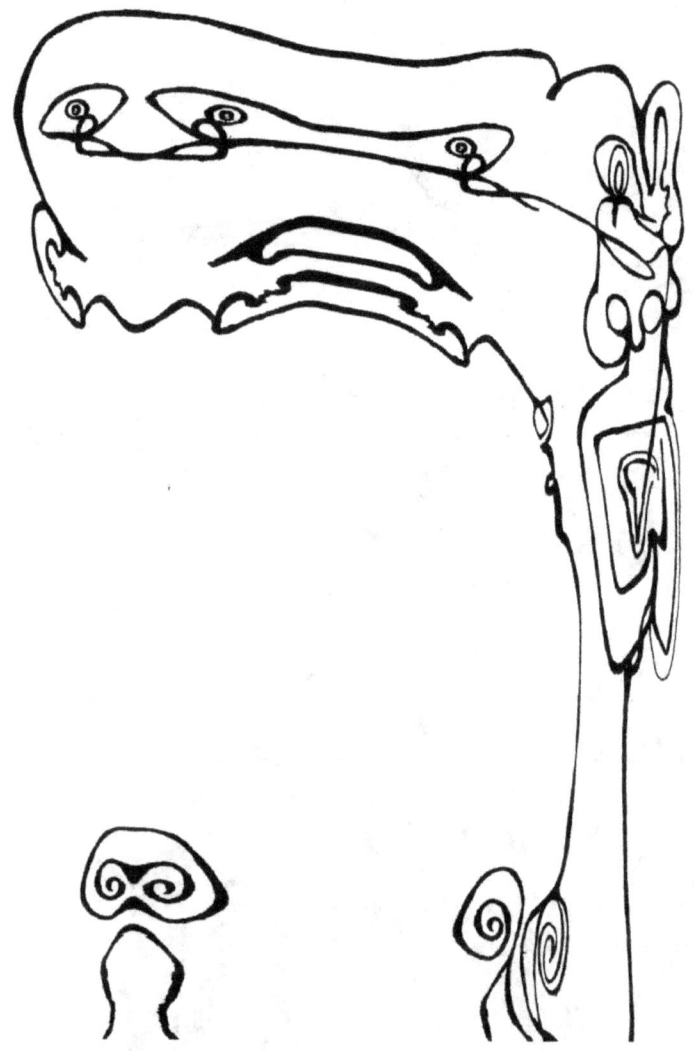

POISED

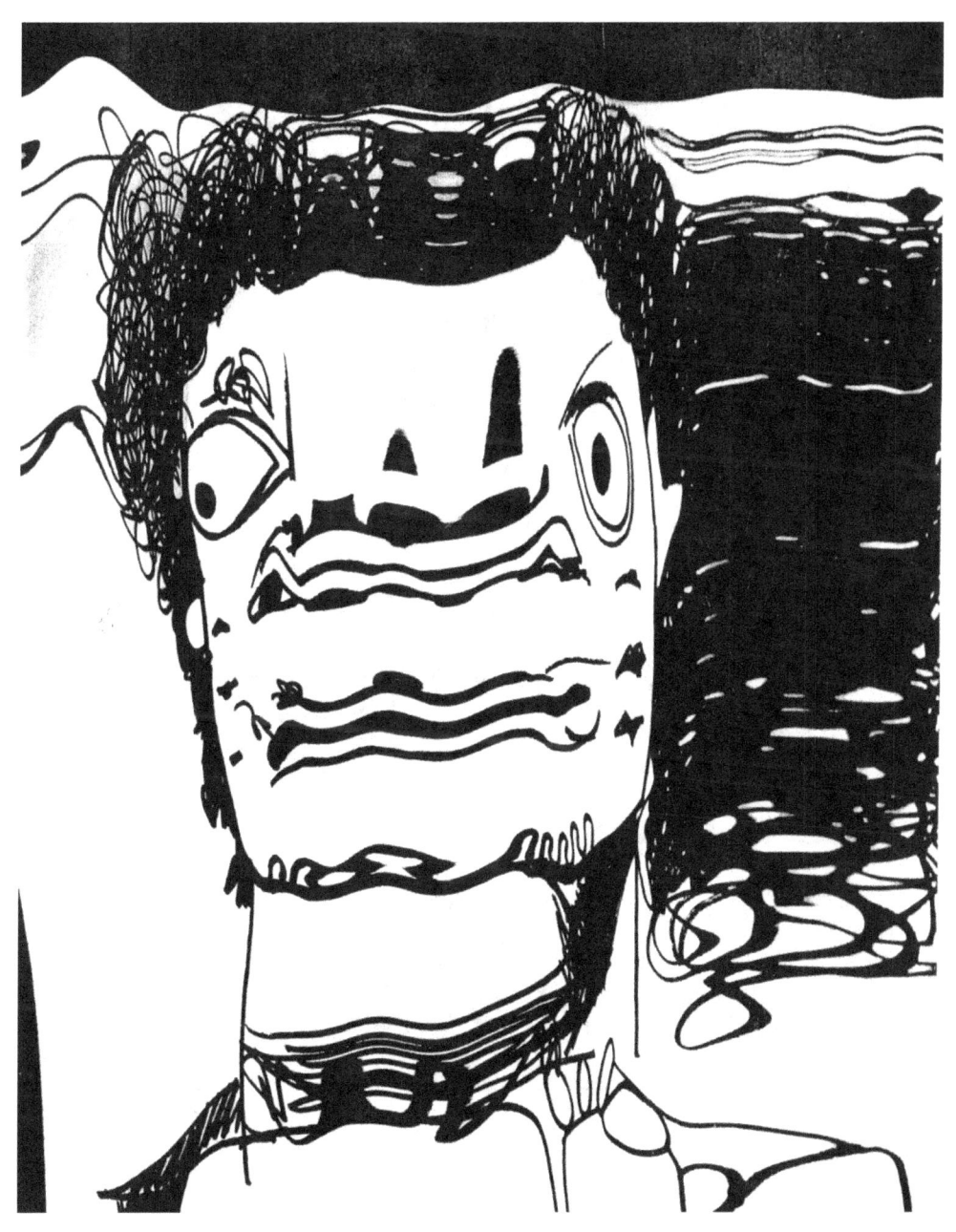

POLYTHEIST

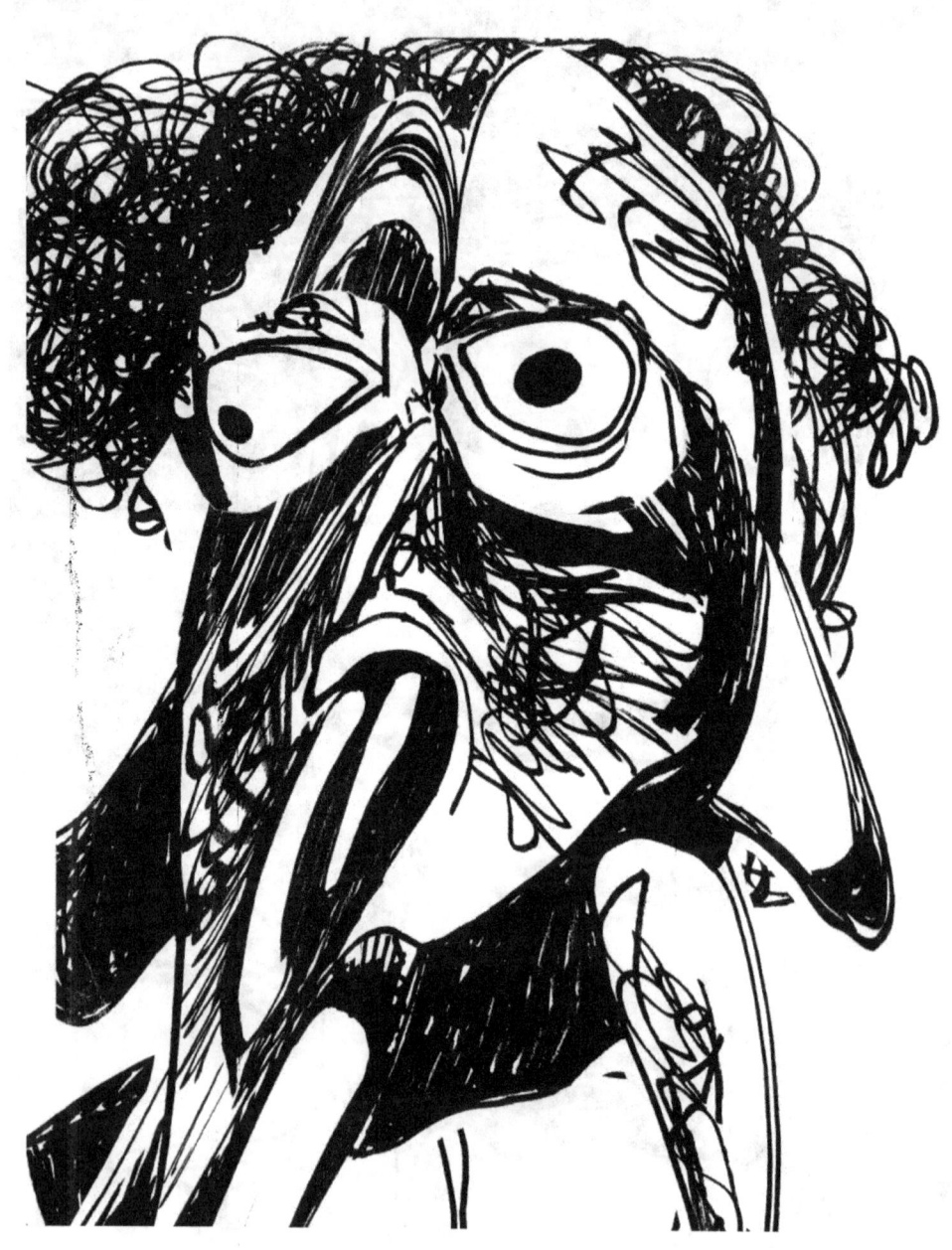

READYMADE

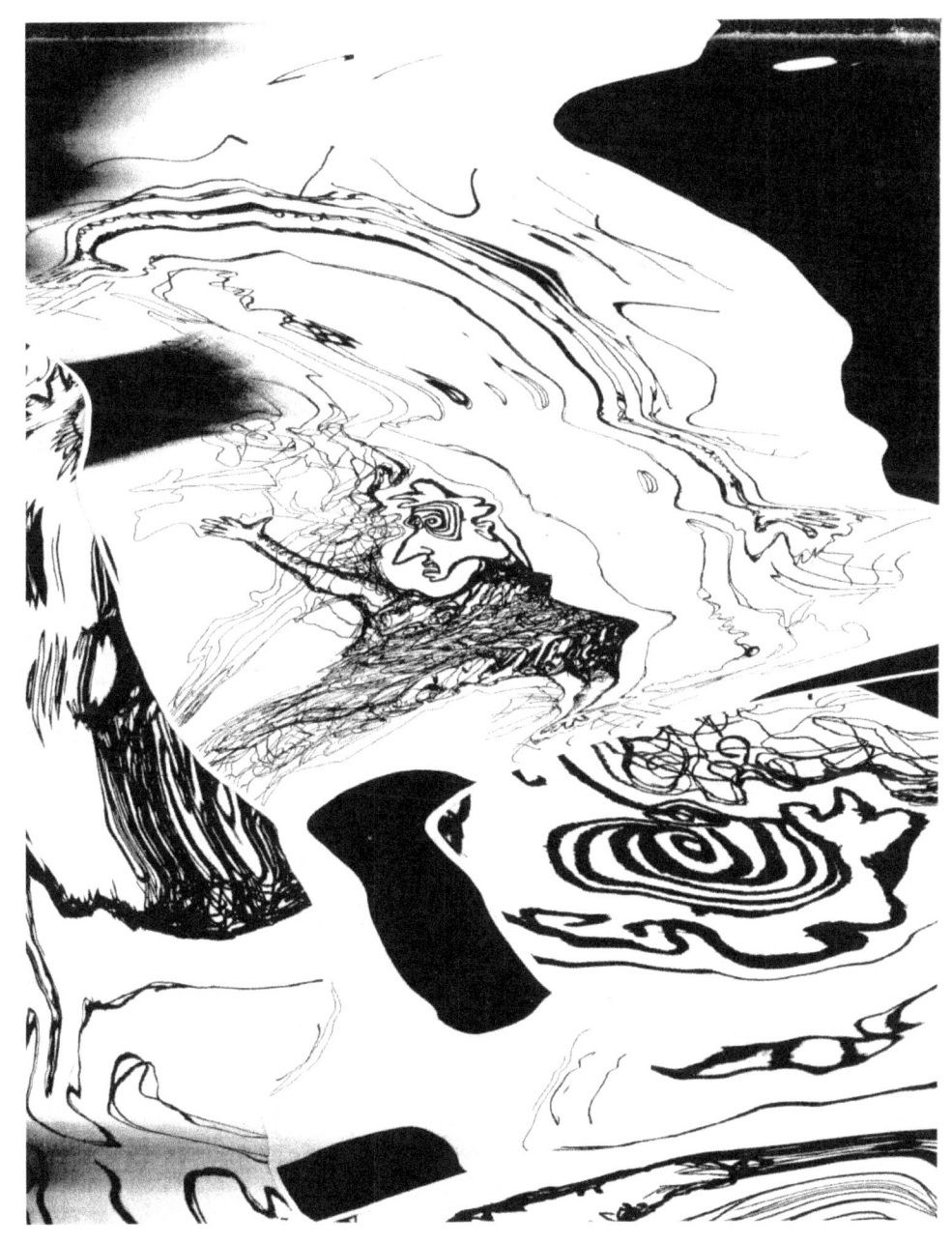

SHROUD SHRUBBERY

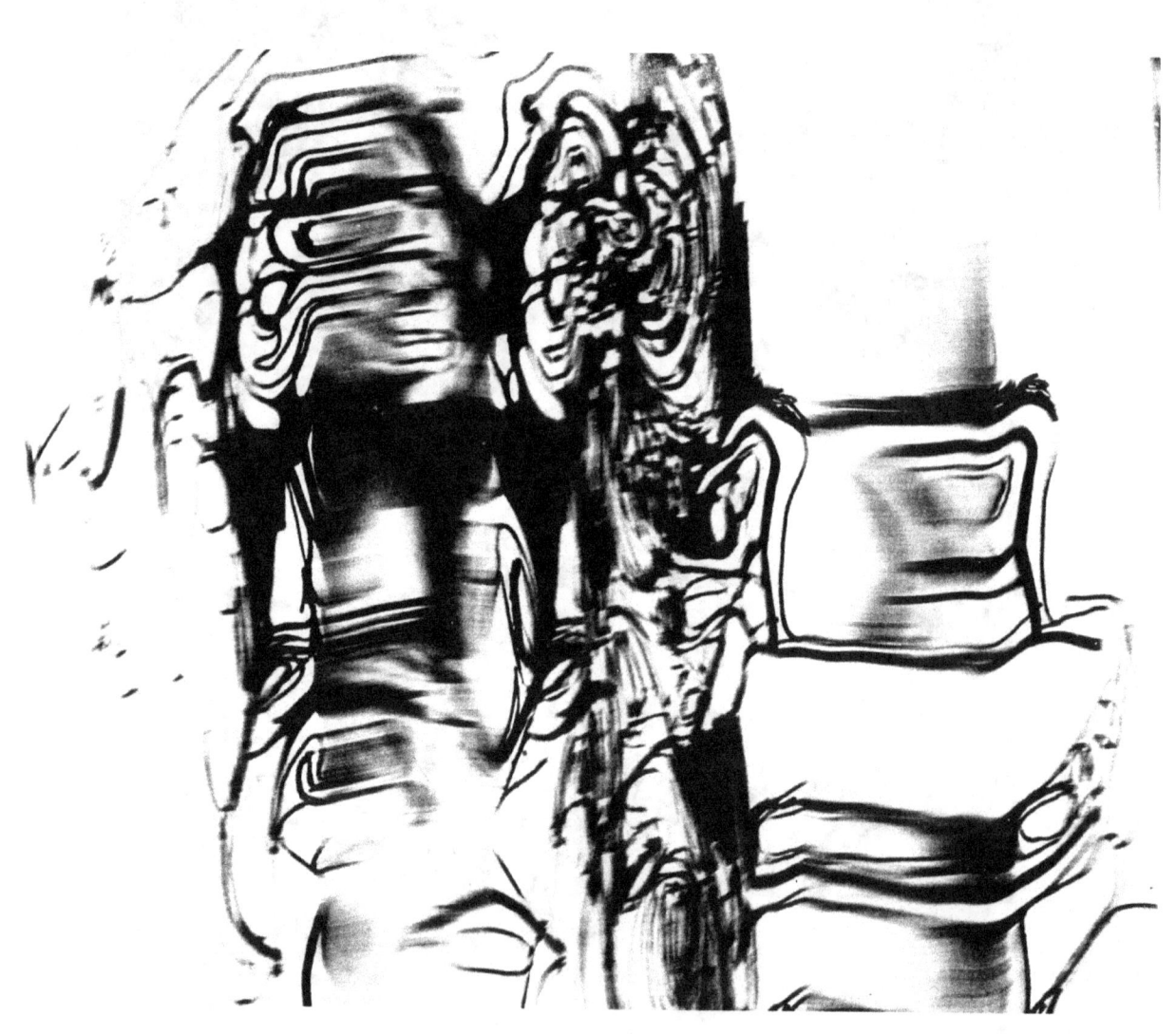

SLUR

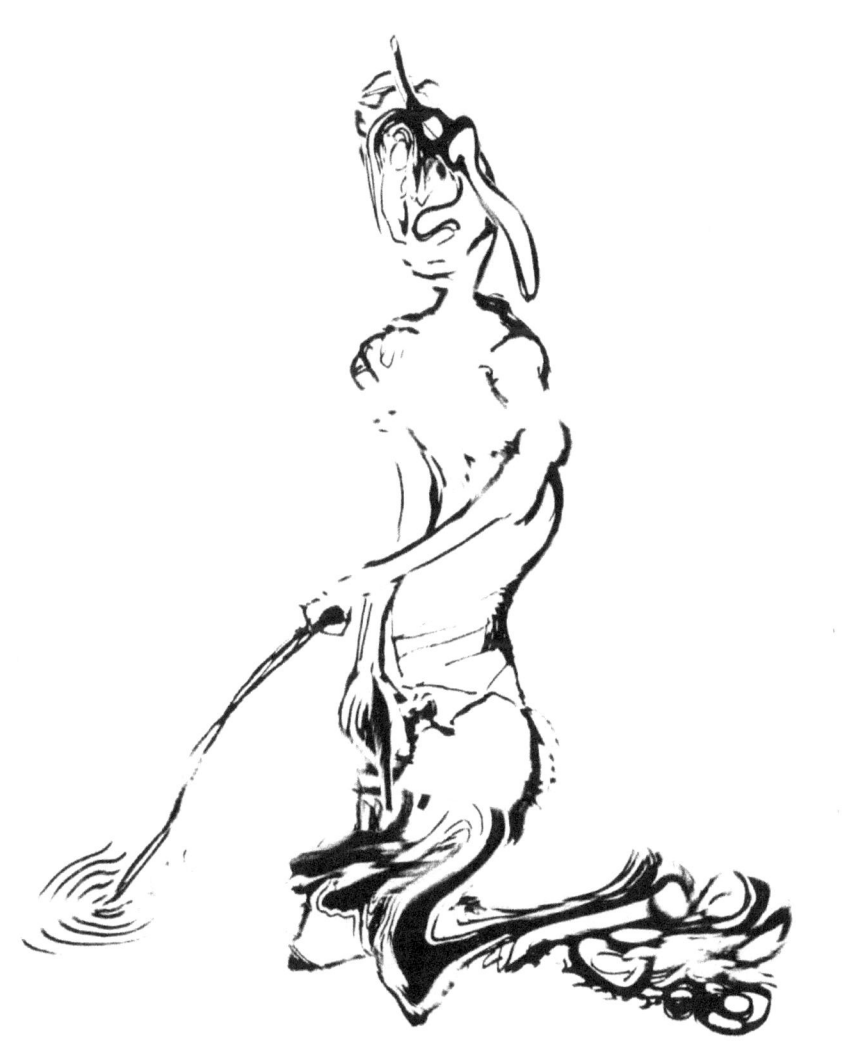

STICKMAN

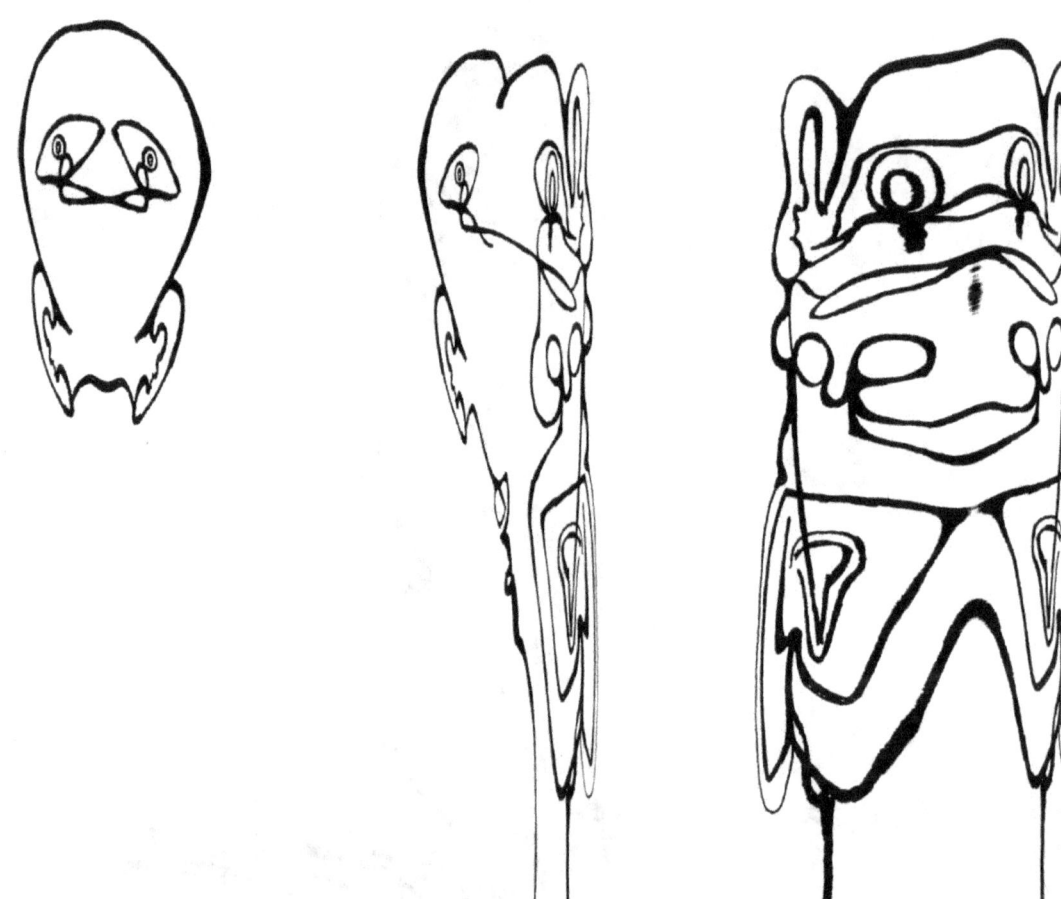

TRINITY

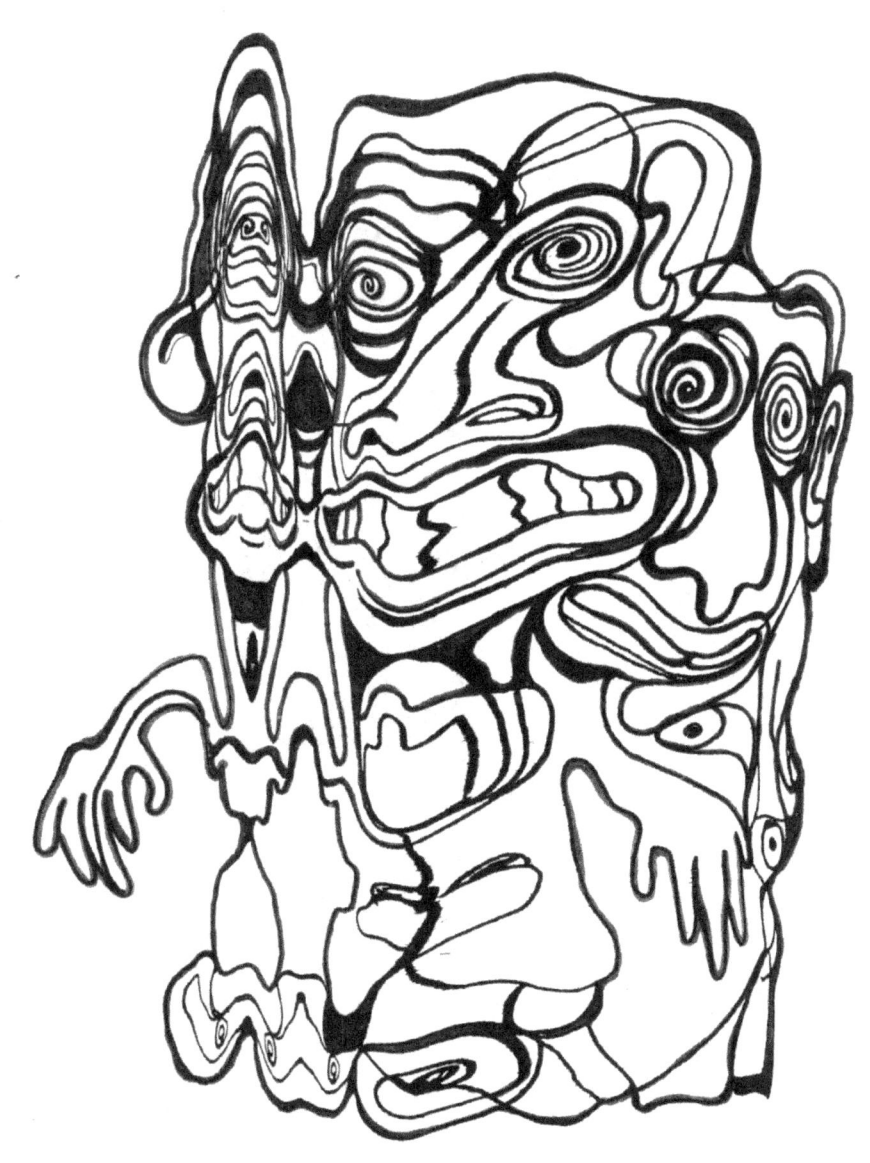

WINDEX WE CAN

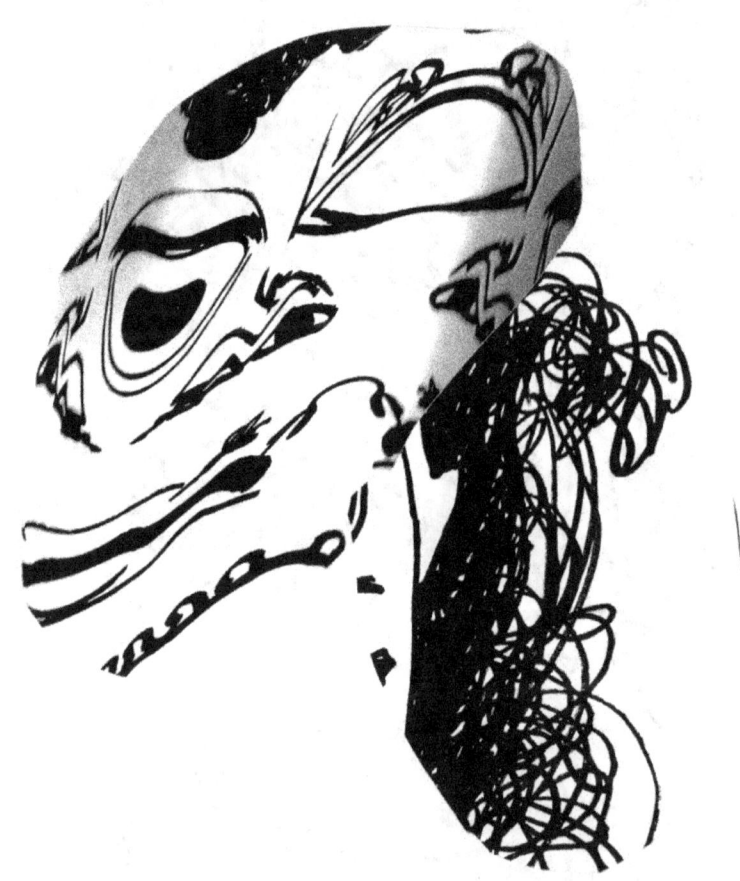

WITCH TIT

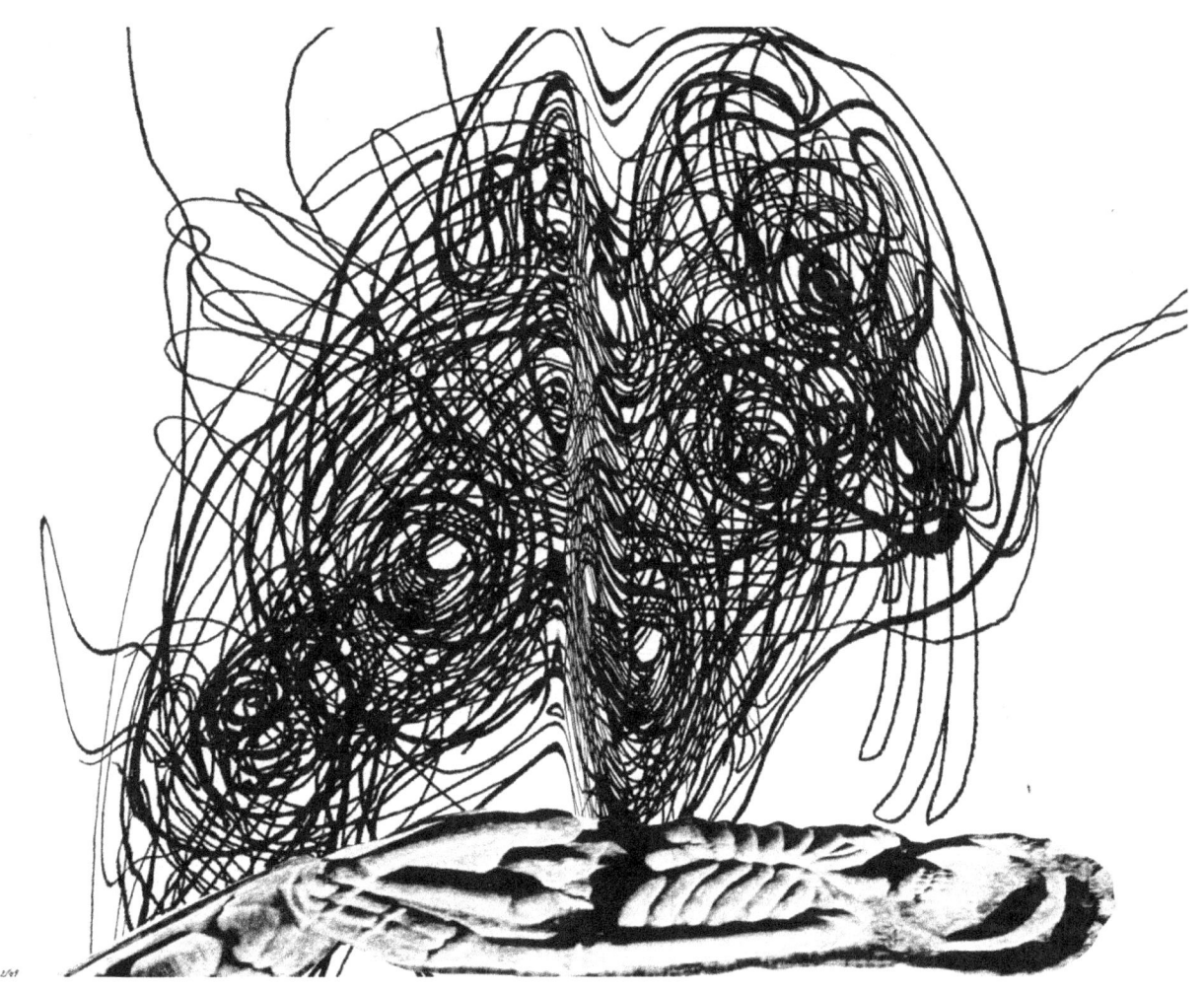

YEARNING

Biographical Information

RC Miller lives in Metuchen, NJ. He is also creator of *Mask With Sausage* and *Pussy Guerilla Face Banana Fuck Nut*, both published by Gobbet. He maintains an art blog via http://visionblues.blogspot.com/

www.ingramcontent.com/pod-product-compliance
Lightning Source LLC
Chambersburg PA
CBHW081735170526
45167CB00009B/3834